Prayer Partnerships
The Power of Agreement

Prayer Partnerships
The Power of Agreement

Ruthanne Garlock and Quin Sherrer

VINE BOOKS
SERVANT PUBLICATIONS
ANN ARBOR, MICHIGAN

Vine Books is an imprint of Servant Publications especially designed to serve evangelical Christians.

Details and circumstances of certain events and some names of persons and locations have been changed to protect individuals' privacy.

Published by Servant Publications
P.O. Box 8617
Ann Arbor, Michigan 48107

Cover design: Keith Sherrer—iDesignEtc., Colorado Springs, CO

01 02 03 04 10 9 8 7 6 5 4 3 2 1

Printed in the United States of America
ISBN 1-56955-254-1

Library of Congress Cataloging-in-Publication Data

Garlock, Ruthanne.
   Prayer partnerships: experiencing the power of agreement / Ruthanne Garlock and Quin Sherrer.
      p. cm.
Includes bibliographical references.
ISBN 1-56955-254-1 (alk.paper)
   1. Prayer. I. Sherrer, Quin. II. Title.

BV215 .G365 2001
248.3'2—dc21

                                                        2001025355

Dedicated to our husbands:
LeRoy Sherrer and John Garlock

And to our faithful prayer partners:
Fran Ewing, Lib Parker, Laura Watson,
JoAnne Bailey, Kerry Bruton, Diane Burwell,
Dee Eastman, Jane Droge, Jane Hansen,
Elizabeth Pichotta, Betty Moore, Bobbye Byerly,
Dottie Sims, Quinett Simmons, Beth Alves,
Cindy Finberg, Jill Griffith, Becky Hicks,
Kay Hoffman, Florence Mukoro,
Cathy Robertson, Keren Stoll,
and Sharon Spencer

Other titles by the authors:

How to Pray for Your Family and Friends
A Woman's Guide to Spiritual Warfare
A Woman's Guide to Breaking Bondages
A Woman's Guide to Spirit-Filled Living
A Woman's Guide to Getting Through Tough Times
The Spiritual Warrior's Prayer Guide
Prayers Women Pray
The Making of a Spiritual Warrior
How to Pray for Your Children
Praying Prodigals Home

Other titles by Quin Sherrer:

Listen, God Is Speaking to You
Miracles Happen When You Pray
Good Night, Lord

Contents

Contents

Introduction

This is the twelfth book Quin and I have written together, although she has authored several other titles on her own. But when Kathy Deering at Servant Publications cast the vision for this book, it seemed to us that the topic of prayer partners begged dual authorship. So right after finishing book number eleven, we launched this project.

"How did you two get started writing books together, anyway?" people often ask.

Since this is a book about partnerships, it seems appropriate to answer that question. In this book we make the point that God Himself, by orchestrating divine appointments and leading us even when we're unaware of it, puts prayer partners together. He does the same for writing partners!

Quin and I first met one blistering summer in 1975 at a writers' conference on the campus of Christ for the Nations Institute in Dallas, Texas. My husband and I were on staff there at the time, and I was the coordinator for the conference. The late Jamie Buckingham, Quin's friend and writing mentor, was our featured speaker. Jamie called Quin and told her she needed to be at this conference, and she came.

I was so busy making sure everyone was housed and fed, the air conditioning was working, and the sessions ran on time, that the conference itself passed in a blur. But I did meet several people that week who became very dear friends. Two, Ann Rosenberg and Beth Alves, became my close prayer partners a few years later. Then thirteen years later, one became my writing partner. Quin.

How did it happen?

Beth Alves and Quin also became friends and prayer partners after meeting at that conference. In 1988 Beth's ministry,
Intercessors International, invited Quin to teach a prayer seminar called "How to Pray for Your Children." Quin's first book
by that title, published by Aglow International, was the basis of
the seminar.

At the time, my mom was greatly burdened for her granddaughter (my niece), who was going through drug rehabilitation. I invited Mom to go with me to this meeting at a guest
ranch in the Texas Hill Country, feeling it would give us some
quality time together. And both of us could learn more about
praying for our children and grandchildren. My long-term
prayer partner, Cindy Finberg, joined us and we three roomed
together.

On the last day of the seminar, Quin came to me with file
folder in hand, saying she needed to find someone to help
with the sequel she was writing to the book from which she'd
just been teaching. The title was to be *How to Forgive Your
Children.* Would I consider it?

My first inclination was to say no. That didn't sound like a
topic I wanted to deal with. But of course I promised to pray
about it.

Then I said, "Quin, I know how writers are—I'll bet you
have a whole boxful of stuff for this project in the back of your
car, don't you?"

"Yes, I do," she said, laughing.

"OK, bring it to my cabin and I'll have a look," I said.

It was a setup, you could say. Or a divine connection. Sitting
on the porch of that ranch cabin, I looked through the material and asked Mom and Cindy to pray with me about it.

Almost immediately I felt the Lord say, "Do it." I looked up to see Cindy grinning at me. I'm pretty sure she knew what His answer would be before I did.

When Quin and I had lunch together in Dallas the following week, I agreed to work on the project. And we've been working on projects ever since.

Why share the details of this story?

Simply to illustrate the way God weaves our lives together, causes us to cross paths with the people He wants us connected with, and uses our partnership efforts to further His kingdom.

Quin and I never envisioned where our small beginning would lead—we simply followed one step at a time. In 1989 we began writing for Servant Publications, and this is our ninth joint project with them.* We know neither of us could have accomplished alone what we've been able to do together. The bonus is that over the years we've become good friends and prayer partners, too.

We pray this book will inspire you to ask the Lord to give you divine appointments and lead you into prayer and ministry partnerships that will enrich your Christian walk and benefit others.

—Ruthanne Garlock
Bulverde, Texas

* In 1998 we took material from the first version of *How to Pray for Your Children*, added new material, plus parts of *How to Forgive Your Children*, to create the revised edition published by Regal. That revised edition counts as two titles for us. See the opening pages of this book for a list of all of our titles.

Chapter One

The Power of Agreement

If two of you on earth agree about anything you ask for, it will be done for you by my Father in heaven. For where two or three come together in my name, there am I with them.

MATTHEW 18:19-20

What comes to mind when you hear the word *agree*? A handshake? A nod of agreement? An oral or written statement to be of one mind about a matter? The business world understands the word in terms of written contracts.

But in the above Scripture, the word *agree* derives from a Greek root from which we get our English word *symphony*. It means to "to sound together ... to be in accord concerning a matter."[1]

Picture in your mind a symphony orchestra. It consists of different types of instruments—some play the melody, some play harmony, some play rhythm. Yet all the musicians follow the same composition, in the same musical key, under the direction of a conductor.

That is a picture of praying in agreement. We may have different styles of praying, but all our prayers are based on the Word of God, under the guidance of the Holy Spirit. Of course, private prayer is a vital discipline for every believer. However, praying about a matter with one or more prayer partners makes a powerful and eternal impact in the spiritual realm.

Be encouraged by the people you'll meet in this book. Some have had miraculous answers to their joint prayers, while others wait in expectant faith. But each of them has learned the power of praying in agreement.

In the following chapters we provide guidelines to help you develop a prayer partnership so you may experience the effectiveness of this type of praying. We will explore various prayer-partner options, including praying with friends, spouses, parents, siblings, and children—either in small clusters of two or three, or in larger numbers. Everything we've learned in the privacy of our prayer closets can be multiplied as we pray corporately.

So put aside any preconceived notions you may have of boring prayer meetings. Let's plunge in and learn how to release the power of agreement while praying with others.

Two Daughters in Agreement

Family problems often divide siblings instead of bringing them together, but in the case of Meg and Gina, a family problem caused them to become prayer partners. Meg traveled from Ohio and Gina from Florida for their parents' anniversary celebration in Illinois. During the visit they were horrified as they observed the screaming and arguing between Mom and Dad—who had reared their six children in a Christian home.

"What has happened? What can we do?" the sisters asked one another.

"As far away as we are from them and from each other, we can't do anything but pray," Gina concluded.

"Yes, we can agree in prayer," Meg offered.

Every Friday morning at eight o'clock they prayed, "Lord, what we want is for You to become top priority in our parents' lives. Come as their Peacemaker. Draw Mom and Dad back to You. In Jesus' name, amen."

After a year of praying, they learned their mother had colon cancer. She was fearful, but finally agreed to radiation treatments.

One day Gina phoned her sister. "I know God did not give her cancer, but He can turn this illness for good in Mom's life. Let's pray that way."

"I agree," Meg echoed.

They kept praying and God moved. Meg got a phone call one night from her mom.

"I want you to know I've come to depend on God through this cancer ordeal," she said. "I haven't done that in ages. I've also found out what a wonderful help your dad can be. We want you kids to come home again soon."

When I visited Meg in Ohio recently, she told me, "Mom has been free of cancer for sixteen years now. And peace and harmony between her and Dad is evident in their home."

The power of praying in agreement is a spiritual dynamic that cannot be explained by logic. We (Quin and Ruthanne) pray in agreement with other intercessors all the time and hear testimonies of its effectiveness everywhere we go.

We see an example in Scripture of the power of agreement when, in obedience to Jesus' instructions, 120 of his followers gathered in the Upper Room to await the gift of the Holy Spirit. They "continued with one accord in prayer and supplication.... And when the day of Pentecost was fully come, they were all with one accord in one place" (Acts 1:14a; 2:1, KJV).

The term *one accord* means "being in agreement, having group unity, having one mind and purpose."[2] It appears more often in the Book of Acts than in any other book of the Bible. God's response to the prayers of agreement in the Upper Room—sending the gift of the Holy Spirit—had such a powerful impact on the world that we continue to see results from it today.

Clearly, the prayer of agreement leads to *results* and *action!*

Don't Give Up Easily!

Ellen and LeeAnn's experience illustrates the value of persevering in prayer, even when the answer is slow in coming.

The two were good friends who enjoyed sharing their dreams, desires, and hopes with each other. Then they decided they would put God to the test to find out if Matthew 18:19 really worked. They began praying together daily Monday through Friday for an hour or two. LeeAnn would drive her daughter to school, then stop at Ellen's house for their prayer time.

"We would stand in the middle of the room praising and giving thanks to God," Ellen said. "We held hands (touching and agreeing) and prayed according to the Word. Though we began to see results right away in many cases, the prayers for our own personal needs often took a little longer to be answered."

Ellen shared just a few of the victories they've seen.

One Monday LeeAnn's aunt called and asked for prayer that she'd find a job. That same day she applied for a position with the local school district. Ellen and LeeAnn prayed in agreement for this need, and on Wednesday the aunt called again. She had just been hired for the position.

Another time they prayed for a friend whose husband had told her he didn't love her anymore and wanted a divorce. He then packed his bags and moved out. The two prayer warriors began binding the enemy's attack against this marriage, and asked the Lord to release love, unity, and oneness into the relationship. Before the week was over the man called his wife to apologize, said he still loved her, and wanted to move back home. Over time the marriage was totally restored.

Ellen and LeeAnn prayed together persistently for months for their own husbands' salvation. Today both men are committed to the Lord and attending church with their wives.

"One day as we were praying in agreement, we began to plead the blood of Jesus over our husbands and children— binding the enemy and asking God to put ministering angels around them and us," Ellen said. "My husband called from the hospital, having fallen off a truck. Some rocks on the ground broke his fall and kept him from hitting the concrete pavement directly. He had a few cracked ribs, but he recovered quickly and was back to work in two weeks. During that time LeeAnn and I kept praying in agreement, and God met all our needs.

"For fifteen years we've been praying together for all kinds of situations. Sometimes it has taken years of persistent prayer to see the answer come, but the prayer of agreement works every time!"

Praying in Agreement Brings a Miracle

When I (Quin) was living in Florida, six of us women met every Monday at 5:30 A.M. at my friend Fran's home to pray extensively for our families. One night we got a call that Fran's thirty-year-old stepson, Mark, was near death with Hodgkin's disease—advanced cancer of the lymphatic system. He also had an inoperable chest tumor. His chances for survival were slim, especially since his problem had gone undiagnosed for six months or more.

Fran, Fran's husband Mike, and Mark's wife accompanied Mark to an Atlanta hospital where his dad had formerly served on the staff. Besides being in pain, Mark was constantly nauseated, and his weight had dropped to 125 pounds. Doctors removed his spleen and did additional biopsies to determine the extent of his problems. They suggested chemotherapy, but it was a long shot. Even if he lived, he would never father children. "God, I so want to live," Mark prayed one afternoon, looking at the dogwood tree blooming outside his window.

How clearly I remember the call from Fran in Atlanta at two o'clock one morning. "Doctors say he can't survive the night," she said through her sobs. I alerted the others in our Monday morning prayer group, and all of us, together with our husbands, got out of bed and began to battle in prayer for Mark's life. "Devil, you aren't having him," we declared. "God is the healer, and by Jesus' stripes Mark is healed! We speak *life* to Mark, not death."

Slowly he began to improve. Doctors began chemotherapy, then finally released him to return to Florida. But life-and-death questions still hung in the air. Even if the drugs worked against the cancer, could he fully regain his health?

On the first Sunday that he was strong enough, Mark went to church with his parents and the entire congregation had a special healing service for him. Over the next six months he received twelve powerful treatments. Despite the extreme nausea, he began putting on weight and, with every checkup, gained more hope. He clung to this verse: "Though you have made me see troubles, many and bitter, you will restore my life again; from the depths of the earth you will again bring me up" (Ps 71:20).

God did just that. Nearly twenty years have passed since Mark's battle with cancer. Those of us in the Monday-morning group who stood with Fran often thank God for our first miracle answer to prayer. Today Mark has two healthy sons and is still praising God for sparing his life.

A Doctor's Prayer Team

Is it important for professional people to have prayer partners, too? Absolutely! Dr. Perry, a chiropractor, has a public practice in the Midwest. He also treats many ministry leaders without charge in what he calls the Gilgal Ministry.

After years of renting a building, he and his wife felt it was time to build their own clinic. Obstacles of every kind lay in their path: red tape over city permits, disagreements with the contractor, lengthy building inspections, and delays due to bad weather. They enlisted their faithful Gilgal prayer partners to help them cover every part of the project with prayer.

"Whenever an obstacle arose—and there were many—our partners prayed for it to be removed," Dr. Perry reported. "They also prayed continually for us to have favor, and God answered. On many occasions we received favor with the city, with our contractor, and even with the telephone company."

Soon even the contractor became aware that the prayer team was at work. Several times he said to the doctor, "Tell those people who pray for you to keep it up. As long as I was working on your clinic, all my jobs went well. Now that your job is finished, everything seems to be falling apart!"

Upon completion of the building, Dr. Perry dedicated it to the glory of God. The clinic continues to be a witness of God's blessing and favor.

Agreement With God

"God wills that we partner with Him in seeing His promises fulfilled," writes Pastor Jack Hayford. "Most promises are not automatically fulfilled apart from prayerful, humble request. He [God] can keep His promises, He wills to keep His promises, but He won't keep His promises—unless people pray. True, He doesn't want us to beg. But equally true is the fact that He wants us to become maturing sons and daughters who increasingly partner with Him in the business of the Kingdom.

"It is by this partnership in prayer that a believer may fulfill Jesus' instructions to pray, 'Thy will be done in earth, as it is in heaven.' The target of our fellowship with Him is to lead us into partnership with Him."[3]

Scripture tells us Jesus was always in agreement with his Father (see Jn 5:19). In like manner, before praying in agreement with a prayer partner about a matter, we should make sure our prayer is according to God's will. Of course, when we pray for a loved one's salvation, we know this is in agreement with His Word. We have His promise: "This is the confidence we have in approaching God: that if we ask anything according to his will, he hears us" (1 Jn 5:14).

One woman shared with us the encouraging results she's seen from praying with other women whose husbands were not believers. This is a prayer they knew was in line with God's will (see 2 Pt 3:9).

"Some of my girlfriends and I were saved and filled with the Holy Spirit about the same time," she wrote. "Two seasoned Christian ladies took us under their wings and taught us about faith, prayer, the Holy Spirit, and believing God's Word. None of our husbands were saved, so we decided to stand on Scriptures for our household. We prayed together every day, believing God for our husbands' salvation. Within a few weeks, one by one, like dominoes falling, our husbands came to know Jesus as Lord and Savior."

Thirty-Year Partnership Bears Fruit

Another woman reflected on years of walking with a prayer partner. In their thirty years together, they've grown to be like-minded in their prayer goals. She wrote:

> We realized this partnering was a threesome: God, Annie, and me. He was always there. If we came together to pray feeling heavily burdened, weary, and discouraged, we always left unburdened and joyful. The answers to prayer came as we walked through some tough situations—a wayward daughter living with a boyfriend, cancer healed (one quickly, another through a long recovery), family rifts reconciled, job transfers, and many moves as our husbands climbed their career ladders.
>
> Annie is a challenger to me. If we see a step we are to take in our studies of Scripture, she is quick to say, "Let's do it." She asks questions that challenge, provoke action, or send me searching for answers. She is a continual support, offering me acceptance, loyalty, and a place to be real, where I know what we share will always be kept in confidence.

Trained and Unified for Battle

As Annie and her prayer partner learned over their thirty years together, battles are not won in a day. Spiritual warfare and natural warfare are alike in many ways. Until soldiers are trained and able to march in rank—in agreement, you could say, with a common goal—they cannot be effective. When we link up with another believer to "march" with us in prayer against our enemy, we need an understanding of Scripture (i.e., training), and we must be in unity. Though Satan opposes God and His purposes for us and our loved ones, the prayer of agreement is a powerful weapon to help defeat the enemy and achieve victory.

Pastor Hayford shares an illustration from the Civil War about the necessity of unity and training. At the beginning of the war, the Northern troops and civilians had a misguided notion about how easy it would be for them to win. He writes:

It is a well-recorded fact that the crowds of civilians followed the troops to the first great battle, carrying picnic lunches and prepared for an outing. They hoped that they would be provided with an enjoyable performance before they packed up their baskets and returned home. The thought of real warfare was not in their minds, and few had any idea of the pain and suffering that would follow in the years to come.

It was a warm day as the Northern soldiers marched toward their first confrontation, and many of them began to lay aside their gear because it was too cumbersome on such a hot day. Soldiers arrived at the front without ammunition and other supplies needed for the battle. Many walked at their own pace rather than trying to stay with their companies.

During that first battle, the North was badly defeated because they were not prepared for a real battle. There was little thought given to actual training or troop discipline, and the strategy was merely to "show up and win the battle."[4]

This picture of undisciplined, independent-minded soldiers contrasts radically with the picture of a well-synchronized orchestra cooperating together to reach a common purpose. How much better to follow the example of the Upper Room believers who "continued with one accord in prayer" until God's response came.

Being in agreement—with each other and with God—is the foundation on which to start. In the next chapter we'll examine the value and positive results you can experience in praying with a prayer partner.

Chapter Two

Finding the Right Prayer Partner

Then those who feared the Lord talked with each other,
and the Lord listened and heard. A scroll of remem-
brance was written in his presence concerning those
who feared the Lord and honored his name.

MALACHI 3:16

Victories seem sweeter when they are hard-won with a prayer partner! Prodigals come home. Life-changing decisions fall into place. Wrenching difficulties give birth to golden character. Every step of the way is more glorious when there is someone with whom to share.

What comes to mind when you hear the words *prayer partners?* Perhaps you think, "That's something others do, but surely not me." Or, "I'd be taking a chance on being misunderstood or hurt." Or you doubt you could find someone you could really trust.

In an era where time is short, relationships hard to come by, and privacy prized, we allow such excuses to prevent us from wanting, seeking, or finding a prayer partner.

When the disciples asked Jesus to teach them to pray, He gave them (and us) a model, which is often called the Lord's Prayer. Notice all the plural pronouns: "Our Father ... give us

27

... forgive us ... lead us not ... but deliver us ..." (Mt 6:9-13). It seems apparent they were expecting to pray together. We don't find the term "prayer partner" in Scripture, but certainly the principle of believers praying together occurs repeatedly.

If you don't yet have a prayer partner, we urge you to keep an open mind as we share stories in this chapter about the value of partnership praying.

The Value of Partnership Praying

Sometimes God chooses a prayer partner for us even when we're not consciously seeking one—which was my (Ruthanne's) experience. I met Cindy in 1979 when my husband, John, and I were speaking for a seminar at her church in a city near us. She was a coleader of the women's ministry sponsoring the seminar.

The following year she learned that John and I and our thirteen-year-old son were taking a seven-month missions trip involving travel to seventeen countries. She wrote me saying she felt led to commit to pray for us specifically during this trip, and that every Wednesday she would fast as well. She prayed for all three of us, but her prayers were mainly focused on me. As I dealt with various challenges during that trip, many times I asked the Lord to speak to Cindy and show her how to pray. When I returned she gave me the diary she had kept during those months, recording how the Lord had led her to pray for specific situations.

In comparing her prayer diary with some of my own notes made during the trip, I was astounded to see the parallels.

This was before the days of instant e-mail prayer alerts, so the only way she knew how to pray was as the Holy Spirit led her. I was humbled to think God cared about me enough to provide such a priceless gift.

Cindy and I began praying together regularly after that, mostly over the phone, though occasionally we would get together to pray. Now almost all of our praying is done by phone. Many times after we've discussed our concerns and prayed about them, I refer to Malachi 3:16 and ask the Lord to receive all our conversation as prayer. Being aware that He is listening to everything we say helps us avoid spiritual pride or harsh criticism and judgment of others. For more than twenty years now, God has knit our hearts and spirits together as we've prayed each other through many trials and victories.

Since I've learned the value of partnership praying, the Lord has added other special friends from various parts of the country who have also become my prayer partners. Though we don't see one another often, I feel free to contact them at any time with a prayer alert, knowing they will pray. And they know I'll do the same for them. These friends have had a part in praying for every book Quin and I have written together, including this one.

Jesus and His Prayer Partners

Jesus placed great value on relationships. He chose twelve special disciples whom He was always teaching, encouraging, and praying for. And within that group, three were particularly close—Peter, James, and John.

Sitting with the twelve disciples for their last Passover meal together, Jesus predicted that one of them would betray Him, and that Peter would deny Him (see Mk 14:18-31). Of course Peter protested loudly that he never would, and the others echoed his declaration. All except Judas, who left to carry out his deal with Jesus' enemies. The rest of the disciples accompanied Jesus to Gethsemane.

Leaving the larger group behind, Jesus asked Peter, James, and John to go a bit farther and watch with Him while He prayed. Even Jesus, in His humanness, had a deep desire for prayer partners.

These three had the unique opportunity to attend the greatest prayer meeting in human history! Jesus returned to find them asleep and asked, "Could you not keep watch for one hour?" (Mk 14:37b). He again went away to pray and came back two different times, only to find them still sleeping. Just then, Judas came with Roman soldiers to betray Him. Peter, James, and John had allowed the moment of opportunity to slip away. The prayer partners Jesus deeply desired to stand with Him disappointed Him.

This poignant vignette makes a powerful statement about the value and importance of prayer-partner relationships. It's possible that, just as Jesus experienced, one or more prayer partners will let you down at some point in your walk with Him. Maybe it won't be intentional, but they will disappoint you.

Effective intercession requires diligence and faithfulness on our part. Pastor Dutch Sheets gives good advice in his book *Intercessory Prayer:*

Let's try to lay down our fears, insecurities and tendencies toward offense. Let's accept the fact that the Scriptures are filled with principles that put responsibility on us, which must be met to receive God's promises. Let's realize this doesn't cancel grace and promote salvation by works. Grace does not imply "no responsibility" on our part.

... Let's cast off all laziness, complacency and apathy. Let's realize we will fall short at times and not feel condemned when we do. *Let's!*[1]

Make a decision ahead of time that it is God Himself on whom you depend—not a lone prayer partner, or even a prayer group. The Lord will never let you down. True, His answers may not always come at the time you expect or even in the way you envision. But He will be there for you. He will never leave you or forsake you.

Don't allow one disappointing experience to rob you of the rich blessing of having a prayer partner. Ask God, in His perfect timing, to lead you into the right relationship.

Changing Patterns for Prayer

One of my (Quin's) most fruitful prayer experiences was praying on the phone with my friend Lib at eight o'clock every weekday morning for about seventeen years. During that time we had seven youngsters between us who were near the same age, so our children were our prayer focus. Just two moms praying for our kids. But we saw some wonderful answers to our prayers.

More recently, since moving from Florida, I've found prayer letters are the best way to convey prayer requests to about a dozen of my prayer partners. My husband, now retired and at home in the mornings, is my closest prayer partner. Don't be surprised if, as seasons of your life change, so may your prayer emphasis. You may recognize a need for different prayer partners—for instance, if you go to work, or move, or your circle of influence changes. That doesn't mean you should give up an "older" prayer partner, but remain open to adapting to the new phase you've entered.

A Good Prayer Partner Holds You Accountable

"A God-given prayer partner can speak the truth to you about areas of weakness she sees as enemy strongholds in your life," Lorene wrote us. "The most profound example of this for me was when Cynthia, my prayer partner, discerned that a spirit of timidity had set up a stronghold in my life. It came disguised as false humility and submission. Because I fully trusted Cynthia's spiritual insight, and knew she was speaking the truth in love, I listened to her. Through our prayers of agreement we confronted the issue, and I was set free. We've learned we can handle one another's humanness and be honest about our feelings without fear of rejection."

Lorene pointed out, however, that sometimes we have to stop and ask, "What is God saying to you about this?" We must be careful about going to our prayer partner instead of to the Lord.

"One time I asked Lorene to pray about a certain situation

and I told her what to pray," Cynthia told us. "She hesitated, which I thought was strange. Then she said she couldn't pray that way. My first reaction was to be offended, but later I understood she was listening to the Holy Spirit for direction. She wanted to pray as He directed and not be manipulated by me. It was a valuable lesson."

Over time Cynthia and Lorene have developed a high level of mutual trust, which frees them to be completely honest about their feelings. Each knows she can't try to "put up a good front" if anything is bothering her. The other one will discern that something's wrong and confront her partner to open up to pray and seek God's guidance in the matter.

Partners in Similar Circumstances

God brought a prayer partner into Janell's life when she began a Sunday school class to minister to women whose husbands weren't serving the Lord.

"It's a hard and lonely walk in the Spirit when you walk with God and your mate does not," Janell wrote us. "For the class, I used the term 'spiritually divided,' because women in this situation actually are divided from their mates as far as the spiritual realm is concerned. In such cases many women struggle just to make it, and others fall away. God birthed within me the determination to walk with Him, and to help others do so as well. He showed me that my husband's decisions, actions, and lifestyle did not have to define what I would do or who I would become. I was to allow the Holy Spirit to be my Counselor, and I was to trust God with my husband, our son, and our futures."

When Janell paired everyone in the class with another woman as a prayer partner, she began praying regularly with Sue. Although Sue was fourteen years younger than Janell, the two connected very well in the Spirit, and their partnership stuck.

"I found that Sue prayed for my family in the same way I did," Janell said. "We could truly be 'in agreement' when we prayed. We always ask the Holy Spirit to lead us as we pray, and He often leads us to pray about things in advance. For instance, once the Lord showed us that He wanted to promote Sue's husband. We prayed that way, and soon he was promoted on his job. Another time the Lord directed us to pray for them to own their own home and not pay rent anymore. We began praying, though it looked utterly impossible that they could buy a home. A year later Sue and her husband were homeowners. It seems the Lord has often answered our prayers 'a year later'!"

For twelve years now Janell and Sue have prayed together, usually by phone, at least once a week. Although Janell may partner in prayer with others from time to time, she considers her partnership with Sue to be a covenant relationship. "I could no more take on another prayer partner at this level than I could take on another husband," she says. When they connect by telephone they catch up on news, then pray in turn as they take everything to the Lord. They find a time, usually in the morning, that fits their lives for that particular week or month, always working around jobs and families and vacations.

"Our husbands are still not saved, but we have not given up believing even this will happen," Janell wrote. "In the meantime both of us are still married, still serving God in leadership capacities, and our children also are serving the Lord. God has done many miracles and answered our prayers again and again. One value of a prayer partner is that what one doesn't recall, the other does. We always have much to praise Him for!"

Partners Despite Transfers

Betty met her prayer partner one Sunday morning when Ann approached her at church and introduced herself as a newcomer to the city. They discovered they had attended the same Bible school, though not at the same time, so they had a common link.

"Because we shared the same teaching, it was good to spend time with one another and not meet a blank stare at some observation about the Scripture," Betty said. "Ann and I met weekly with another lady and enjoyed the time reviewing our sermon notes, discussing how the truth applied to our lives, and praying for one another and our families. We set goals for ourselves, then held one another accountable to strive for those goals."

When Betty's husband was transferred to Los Angeles about five years later, she and Ann sadly parted, not knowing what God had in store for them. But four months later Ann's husband accepted a position as CEO of a company in the same area. "Blessed beyond measure, we resumed our weekly meetings for almost a year," Betty recounted.

Ann reports that during their time in California she went through a crisis of faith while writing a paper for a theology course she was taking. It seemed to her the Christian experience had been reduced to establishing a theological position, then being able to prove it through Scripture. The sense of a personal relationship with God and knowing His presence was not there for her. Then the two prayer partners spent the night together while their husbands were out of town, and Ann shared her frustrations.

"Let's pray," Betty responded.

"How can I pray?" Ann asked. "I have no faith. What must I do?"

Betty was quiet for a time. Then she replied softly, "Ann, I don't know any other way. You must choose to believe God first. Everything else will follow."

"I was melted," Ann reported, looking back on the experience. "I knew it was God speaking through her, and those words became a foundational truth in the area of faith for me. Praying together has always put everything in an eternal perspective. Sometimes that is hard for me to do alone. Years of praying with Betty have made a tremendous difference."

When Jim was transferred again, Betty and Ann kept in touch by writing and occasionally phoned. After a few years their husbands' jobs caused them to move back to Texas. Now both couples are retired, living less than a hundred miles from one another.

"We are close enough to meet about once a month," Betty said. "The wonder of it all is that we can share our news, discuss what we're currently reading, and what God is saying to each of us. Then we pick right up with precious prayer time as though there had been no separation. We marvel at the way God has allowed our paths to cross through our many transfers, and continually thank Him for this blessing."

Waiting for God's Timing

"I have many funny stories about my misguided attempts to make friends and build the life I thought God had for me," Debbie said of the frustrations she faced when she moved from a small town to a large city. "Besides seeking a prayer partner, I also had hoped to find a weekly prayer group to pray with. The first person I thought would make a good prayer partner backed out after we'd gotten together only once. Then I met another 'friend' at church and called her one day to ask about a prayer group. The conversation went something like this:

"Hello, Melissa [not her real name]. This is Debbie. I'm hoping you may be able to help me find a ladies' prayer group that meets to pray together about once a week."

"Sorry, uh, Debbie?" (*She's trying to remember who I am. I get the feeling I didn't make such a great impression on her ...*) "Please excuse me—I'm getting ready to leave. I'll have to call you later."

"So, Melissa, where are you headed to this morning?" (*It's really sad I was so desperate that I actually asked her this question. She is obviously very busy and I can tell she wants to leave, even as I try to continue the conversation.*)

"I'm leaving right now to go to a prayer meeting! I'm late already. Gotta go!"

"That's exactly what I'm calling about! Do you think I could get more information about this prayer meeting? Is it open to anyone? What do you pray about?"

"Uh, well, it's just a group of ladies ..." (*more sounds of preparation to leave as soon as she can get off the phone!*) "We, uh, pray for our families and for the city. Uh, have I met you?"

"Yes, Melissa, we met at church! In Sunday school class!"

"Sorry, gotta go, my ride's here!" (*Obviously she did not even hear my response, did not remember me at all.*)

"Though I couldn't see it at the time, God used what I thought was the hardest season of my life to strengthen my bond with Him," Debbie concluded. "In later years I allowed God to lead me into genuine Holy-Spirit-breathed relationships in this city. It is my home, and I love it now. Over the years I've had several extremely successful prayer-partner relationships— long-term, short-term, and project-oriented. Some will probably be eternal, but it's all about Jesus. I've never forgotten what I learned during that sweet season of being shut away with the Lover of my soul."

Quin's Divine Appointment

I met my prayer partner, Fran, through one of those God-arrangements. After my husband took early retirement from NASA, we moved to northwest Florida to be closer to my mom. LeRoy worked for a construction firm until we could get the children out of college. I'd been willing to make the move clear across the state, but I knew that more than anything else, I'd miss my two trusted prayer partners: Lib, who prayed with me every weekday morning for five minutes, and

Laura, my more mature prayer partner, who got together with me twice a month.

After we moved, I prayed daily for the right prayer partner. One day while attending our new church, I observed a woman pushing her husband in a wheelchair. She had the most loving countenance. A big smile that melted my heart. I felt God say, *Ask her.* When I finally gained enough courage to ask her if we could pray together on a regular basis, she said she'd pray about it and let me know.

A few weeks later she told me she had asked four other women to meet at her home on Monday mornings at 5:30 A.M. and I could be a part of that group. Our prayer times were focused only on our families.

We'd arrive to the aroma of coffee topped with whipped cream in Fran's kitchen. Grabbing a cup, we'd each go into the living room to pray. What I immediately liked about this intimate group is that we didn't tell one another our problems or express how we thought we ought to pray. We just immediately launched into prayer, telling our heavenly Father what was on our hearts about our family.

I often walked the boundaries of the room as I prayed; Ginger usually stretched out on the couch and sometimes fell asleep; Susan took her place on the ottoman; Fran had her favorite big blue chair; Claire sat rocking gently in the glider; Carol liked sitting on a pillow on the floor. As we prayed together, I felt I got to know these women and their families in a deeper way.

Fran and her husband, Mike, had been led to the Lord by famous Dutch evangelist Corrie ten Boom. Later, when Corrie had spent time at their home writing some of her books, she had also mentored them in prayer. Now Fran was mentoring us.

After our hour of prayer, four of the women left to get their families off to school or work. Fran and I spent another hour together, usually going out for breakfast, but always praying specifically for each other's families. Our group prayed regularly like this for three years and saw many turnarounds in all our families. As LeRoy and I attended Mike's Bible study for the ten years we lived there, our friendship deepened. At least twice a year we go back to have our spiritual batteries recharged.

During those years I learned that when one is down, it's such a comfort to have others stand in faith and prayer to encourage you. One of my favorite Scriptures talks about a prayer partner at the church in Colossae. Paul wrote, "Epaphras, who is one of you and a servant of Christ Jesus, sends greetings. He is always wrestling in prayer for you, that you may stand firm in all the will of God, mature and fully assured" (Col 4:12).

That's what Fran did for me then and continues to do for me now. She wrestles in prayer that I may stand firm and be mature.

Obstacles That Prayer Partners Encounter

Some women feel so overwhelmed and shamed by the problems in their lives, they're afraid to open their hearts to anyone, even to ask for prayer.

Brenda found herself in this dilemma a few years ago when she finally faced the reality that her married daughter was addicted to hard drugs. The daughter got involved in an affair and moved in with a friend, leaving her two-year-old son with his father, who also was a drug addict. Finally Brenda broke down in tears at church one Sunday morning when Patty, a longtime friend standing nearby, gave her a hug. Patty invited her to a new prayer group she had just started called "The Encouragers."

At last Brenda shared her distress with these women, and they prayed for her and her family. The Lord put other praying women in Brenda's life, and she began a new quest for a deeper relationship with God. "The 'pruning' really is painful, but how could I bear fruit without it?" she said. "Never again will I be flippant with someone when their hearts are broken and say, 'Oh, you've got to have faith and believe God.' Today my daughter is remarried and delivered from drugs, and we have a wonderful relationship. I'm so grateful to God, and to those who prayed for me through those years of anguish."

As in any spiritual endeavor, the enemy seeks to put obstacles in our way when we ask God to direct us to the right prayer partner. It's important to look to Him and trust His timing, recognizing that He wants to be included in any prayer partnership. He is jealous and wants to set the agenda so that it remains God-centered. These are some of the obstacles you may encounter:

1. *Wanting to quit, when you feel you've prayed for ages and have seen no outward results.*

2. *Feeling betrayed—by God, or by a prayer partner.* When we give in to disappointment, rejection, or disillusionment, we're saying, "I just can't trust anyone, not even God."

3. *Believing God has let you down by not answering prayer in your time frame or in the way you had envisioned.* Perhaps things got worse, not better, after you began praying with someone. Jo admitted that when she gathered five women to pray with her they had no victories to report for some time. In fact, at first, each time they prayed for a healing, the person got worse. Discouragement could have caused them to quit, but it didn't. The day came when they witnessed a miraculous healing in answer to their persistent prayers.

4. *Feeling your prayer partner doesn't rate your request as seriously as you do—or makes light of it.* One despondent woman felt her prayer partners were impatient for her to get over her depression so they could pray for the lost and dying—what they considered the "really serious" cases.

5. *Fatigue, guilt, and condemnation.* The enemy will invade your thought life to tear at your self-worth and use guilt as a weapon. "This is what you should have done or should have said to him ..." a prayer partner may have said in a condemning tone. Guilt and condemnation, brought on by insensitive judgments, are heaped on top of your fatigue. You wonder if you can ever pray with a prayer partner again.

6. *Sin. Plain old sin.* Afraid to be transparent with a prayer partner, you fail to "confess your sins to each other and pray for each other so that you may be healed" (Jas 5:16a). This keeps a wall between you and your

prayer partner. Yet when you're honest in sharing, your prayer partner can usually pray for you with more compassion than anyone else.

7. *Being unequally yoked in the Lord.* Different points of view over minor issues should not be a major hindrance, but when doctrines differ considerably, it is hard to pray in agreement. A faithful prayer partner will hold you accountable if you begin straying toward a questionable teaching. Both partners must strive to keep the prayer relationship based on biblical truth.

The Power of Teamwork

As we were finishing this book, I (Ruthanne) happened to watch the 4 x 400 women's relay race on television during the 2000 Olympic Games. In this event each of the four team members runs one 400-meter lap, then passes the baton to a teammate.

Four highly skilled runners represented the United States. Some of the four had won medals in previous events, but not one had taken a medal in the individual 400-meter event. Yet as a team they won first place and took home gold in the 4 x 400 relay. Together they accomplished what no single one of them had been able to do independently.

In the postevent interview, each of the four credited her teammates for giving their best; some even publicly thanked God for helping them. The synergism of working together and encouraging one another gave them the impetus to win.

Immediately I thought of what we said at the beginning of this chapter: "Victories seem sweeter when they are hard-won with a prayer partner!" Your spiritual battle will seem far less daunting when you have a partner or prayer team members to strengthen you and spur you on to victory.

Now let's explore the possibilities and challenges of teaming in prayer with your spouse.

Chapter Three

Making Your Spouse
Your Prayer Partner

Though one may be overpowered by another, two can withstand him. And a threefold cord is not quickly broken.

ECCLESIASTES 4:12, NKJV

M e? Pray with my husband? Are you kidding?"

We often hear comments like this in conversations with women we meet while traveling around speaking at retreats or conferences.

Both of us pray with our husbands on a regular basis, recognizing that a wife and husband, praying in agreement with God's will, create a threefold cord. We derive spiritual strength from this union, yet we fully appreciate how difficult praying together can be for some couples.

I (Quin) will never forget how LeRoy and I got started praying together—almost reluctantly, I'm afraid.

Our pastor at the time, Peter Lord, challenged the men of the congregation to pray with their wives at least once during the following week. He explained the importance of the prayer of agreement, using biblical examples. Then he teased the men, saying he would embarrass them the next Sunday by asking those who had not prayed with their wives to stand up. LeRoy and I prayed together once that week, and at the pastor's suggestion, twice the next week, until we gradually built up a daily habit.

Now when we pray together every day, we settle into our special blue chairs, Bibles in hand. LeRoy leads out by taking authority over "principalities and powers" that would try to thwart God's plan for our family members. He always worships the Lord, thanking Him for His mercy, grace, and for a good night's rest. Then he goes boldly before the throne of God on behalf of our family, calling out the names of our children, in-law children, and grandchildren—even stating the addresses of their homes as he asks God to station His angels about the houses and vehicles. Then he asks the Lord's presence, power, provision, protection, and direction for each of them for that day.

We have a list of people we pray for daily besides our family members: our pastor and his family, five neighbors, sick friends, and regular prayer partners. On certain days we pray for local, state, and national officials. We ask God's blessing on the businesses who employ our adult children. We pray that our grandchildren's teachers will teach with kindness, and will help them develop to their full potential. We also pray for safety for those grandchildren and their classmates, while in school and while going back and forth.

When LeRoy finishes, I recite certain Scriptures that we've prayed for our children for years. From time to time I will read different verses directly from the Bible, but usually I pray:

- That the Spirit of the Lord will rest upon [naming each one] ... the Spirit of wisdom, understanding, counsel, power, knowledge, and the reverential fear of the Lord.
- That our children and grandchildren [name them], like Jesus, will keep increasing in wisdom (mental) and stature (physical) and in favor with God (spiritual) and men (social).
- That our children may walk in a manner worthy of the Lord, to please Him in all respects.
- That all our children shall be taught of the Lord and great shall be their peace.[1]

Some spouses struggle to make time to pray together, but we've found early morning works best. Not every household can do this. It is sometimes hard for us as we have a four-year-old grandson living with us right now. He often gets up earlier than we do and begs for Papa LeRoy's attention. Sometimes he curls up in his papa's lap while we pray, but he is usually too squirmy to last through our entire prayer time. In times of crisis, LeRoy and I sometimes pray together several times a day, crying out for God's intervention. Our prayers of agreement are a defense against the enemy's attacks on our family.

What If Both Don't Agree?

Of course, couples don't always agree on how to pray about a given situation, or how to determine God's will in a matter. In this case, how do we come to a place of agreement?

I (Ruthanne) encountered this several years ago as I felt a

stirring in my spirit about moving away from Dallas, where we had lived for more than twenty years. When I brought up the idea to John, he figured I was just tired of living in an apartment on the Bible school campus where he was teaching. He already was planning to give up full-time classroom work and devote more time to ministry travel. But still, he felt staying in Dallas was the logical thing to do—mainly because of easier airline connections. "Let's just look for a place in the Dallas area where we can have more privacy," he suggested.

But I wasn't interested in that. I quickly realized the whole idea needed lots more prayer. I stopped talking about it, and began asking God to reveal His perfect plan to both of us, and to lead us into agreement concerning it. We were praying together regularly during this time, but I avoided bringing up the topic in our prayer time.

Then we went on vacation to the Hill Country area of Texas, near San Antonio, and John agreed—without much enthusiasm—to look around for property for sale. Over the next year or so we made several more trips. Finally we found what we felt was an ideal seven-acre plot of land with huge oak trees and a wonderful panoramic view. We bought it, still not sure whether or not we would build or just keep it as an investment.

Gradually, John became more and more interested in building a new home, which we had never done before. We prayed together about the project, asking God for guidance in settling on a house design and a builder, and for His timing. In studying the surveyor's drawing one day, John noticed that our piece of land had an unusual winglike shape. It was his idea to name the place "Angelwing."

Almost three years passed from the time we found a piece of property until we moved into our log home. But when we made the move, we were in total agreement that this was a God thing, and that the timing was perfect. Not that it was easy—nor that I coerced John to do it my way. Together we sought the Lord, followed His leading a step at a time, and adjusted our own desires to suit His plan.

John still keeps a very busy schedule ministering overseas and in the U.S.—he just flies out of San Antonio instead of Dallas. And I travel with him as often as other duties allow. We are continually thankful to God for providing this secluded, restful place that is ideal for meditating and writing, and has become such a refuge for us. Neither of us would have it any other way.

Recently I asked John just how his change of mind came about. "Well, it wasn't so much a change of mind as a change of heart," he said. "Although living in the Dallas area makes better sense in human terms, what seems right in the natural isn't always right in God's plan."

Both of us are thrilled that God led us here, and we love living among the oak trees and the deer. But we also feel He has a larger purpose in it all that we don't yet understand. We continue to pray together that God will reveal His plan to us in the days ahead.

Creating Intimacy and Spiritual Wholeness

In their book *When Couples Pray Together,* authors David and Jan Stoop share insights on how a couple can establish spiritual intimacy through their prayer partnership. They write:

We have found that a sense of spiritual intimacy is gained as we, as a couple, seek to restore in our marriage those things that were lost for Adam and Eve back in Genesis. We want to regularly confront not only the shame, defensiveness, and fear that any two people are going to encounter in a marriage, but also seek to repair the brokenness that came as a result of sin, between us as a couple and in our relationship with God.

... A number of couples commented on the fact that as they prayed together and built a greater sense of spiritual intimacy, they also were able to experience a greater sense of physical intimacy. [These comments were taken from the authors' survey of couples who pray together.]

... Physical intimacy is, at its most basic level, a beautiful form of communication. If a husband and wife are not communicating verbally, that lack of communication will soon affect their physical relationship.

... What many couples reported to us was that through praying together daily, they were able to open areas of communication with each other that had been blocked previously.... When a couple kneels to pray together, the glory of God is there with them! What an awesome, intimate, glorious occasion![2]

Bobbie told us that after twenty years of marriage, she and her husband were in the process of getting a divorce when the Lord intervened. Each of them had grown up in a Christian home, and outwardly they maintained the façade of being a Christian family and workers and pillars in the church. But it was just that—a façade. Underneath, each one pursued his or her own agenda, continually struggling to establish their "rights" in the relationship. Finally, they yielded to the power of the Holy Spirit and allowed the Lord to be their mediator. She writes of the results:

> Like the example of the triangle, with God being at the top, the closer we came toward Him from our individual angles, the closer we were to one another. In our times of greatest stress and loss, we found the comfort and peace only God can give by kneeling together in His embrace as He wrapped us in the blanket of His love. In the midst of our most heated disagreements, we find that kneeling together before the Lord brings the oil of His presence on our troubled waters. We can dare to believe in one another because He believed in us, and He is our mediator.
>
> Now we have a wonderful foundation for each day as we fling ourselves into His open arms every morning. There we establish a fresh beginning with the Lord and with one another. In having this three-way "chat" with the Lord each day, we really have come to know the tenderness, the vulnerability, the childlike innocence, the needs, fears, strengths and weaknesses of each other. And we have become more protective of one another. Our grandchildren know the daily "drill." When they sleep over, if they get up early, they join us in the morning huddle.

Opposites Attract

When Dianne and Charles married they knew the Lord wanted them to be prayer partners, but they faced many challenges. It was Charles' first marriage, but Dianne's second, and she had two teenage children still living at home. They had lots of prayer needs!

The two met at a single adults group in a nondenominational church. But Charles had come from a highly structured liturgical church background, whereas Dianne had a more varied background in several different Christian groups. Finding a comfortable way to pray together was anything but easy for them!

"Charles liked to sit and pray silently or very quietly, and I loved to walk around and pray aloud, sometimes singing or shouting," she said. "He thought my prayers were too loud and emotional, and conversely, I felt his prayers were too short and insensitive. At times I would actually interrupt his prayers, instructing him on how he ought to pray and say it correctly."

In retrospect, Dianne realizes she expected prayer times with her husband to be like earlier experiences she had had praying with women partners whose style of praying was like her own. It seemed praying with them had usually brought quick and exciting answers. But finally she admitted it was her pride and critical judging of Charles—not his quiet ways—that were hindering answers to their prayers.

"For years it was a struggle every time we tried to pray together," Dianne said. "I usually ended up being frustrated—a nice word for angry—and impatient. At one point I actually gave up wanting to pray with him, but the way I avoided prayer times with my husband was ungracious and unloving."

In the normal course of things, it seemed impossible for Dianne and Charles to resolve their differences regarding prayer. But God found a way. The turning point came when the two attended a series of Bible classes on marriage.

"The Lord helped me understand that a voluntary role of submission to my husband was God's plan to bring about a full reconciliation of our unity with each other," Dianne said. "This simply meant I must give up trying to lead him or teach him how to pray! I also realized that I shouldn't substitute prayer time with others at the neglect of prayer with my husband.

"A key factor that brought us into harmony in prayer was the operation of the fruit of the Holy Spirit in Charles. He never gave up, never rejected me, and never stopped reaching out to pray with me. He was the 'approved one' in God's eyes, and I, who thought I was so powerful in prayer, was the immature one. How prideful I was, and how lacking in the fruit of the Spirit toward my dear husband."

Dianne reports that she and Charles now experience tremendous unity in their marriage. And they're seeing such wonderful answers to prayer in their family and in their ministry they can hardly keep track of them all.

Your Prayers Are Important

Kathy, our editor for this book, told us how she and her husband decided on their wedding night to begin praying together. For twenty-eight years they've not missed a night of praying together just before going to sleep. If they're separated because of travel, each still prays for the other at bedtime. If one is too sick to pray, the healthy one prays for both.

"We usually go to bed at the same time," she writes, "but even when we don't, the one who is first to retire seeks out the night-owl spouse for a moment of prayer together.

"Once, a few years ago, I wondered whether perhaps our prayers had become too routine to be effective. So often we used the same phrases. So often we were incoherent with fatigue. Sometimes, especially when all four children were small, I would ask my husband, 'Did we finish praying?' because I had fallen half asleep as he prayed. It just seemed kind of flat, so I asked God to show me if we needed to do something different, like maybe pray sitting up (we usually prayed lying in bed side by side). When I asked God this question, I heard His loving rebuke immediately and clearly in my mind: 'YOU HAVE NO IDEA HOW IMPORTANT YOUR PRAYERS ARE!' God's voice was so startling and clear that I reported it to Mike, and we have never since questioned the value of our prayers.

"Because we pray together daily about simple matters, we have found that when bigger troubles strike, we are well equipped to pray together. We have prayed our way through life-threatening illnesses, the severe mental illness of a family member, seven years of infertility, three miscarriages, sudden unemployment, financial trials, major decisions, the deaths of parents and friends, and the teenage rebellion of one of our children."[3]

Praying in Agreement for Your Children

Tammy and Dave, who pray together regularly for their children, have seen the power of prayers of agreement in the lives of their three daughters. Liz, the eldest, had decided at an early age exactly where she wanted to go to college. But when an older girl in their church went away to this same school, she experienced a miserable roommate situation. Some nights she would stay in the school library as long as possible to keep from going back to her dorm.

Two years before Liz graduated from high school, her parents began to pray for God's choice for her college roommate. "It is so important for parents to be in agreement for the lives of their children," Tammy said. "I've always believed God has placed them in our hands to pray for them, and to diligently teach them about the things of God. So Dave and I prayed in advance that God would provide Liz a godly roommate who would reinforce her Christian walk."

The day came when they loaded their daughter and her belongings into their van and drove to the school. When they got to Liz's assigned dorm room, her roommate had already moved her things in. There on the desk lay her Bible and a devotional book. Clearly, God had answered their prayers.

"The similarities between Liz and her roommate are amazing," Tammy said. "She comes from a family of all girls, just like Liz, and even her father's name is the same as my husband's. The girls attend church together and have the same major—they're now seniors and have been roommates all through college. We think this young lady is really special, and we're so grateful God answered our prayers."

Praying Together Through Sorrow

A major reason it's helpful for couples to pray together regularly is so that when difficulties and sorrows come, as they inevitably do, a prayer foundation already is established. The enemy, knowing that prayer often is the glue that holds you together when problems of all kinds try to tear you apart, battles to keep you from praying together. But whatever obstacle the enemy brings can be overcome through love and persistence.

Lee Ezell, an author and speaker, shares her story of learning how to pray with her late husband, Hal:

When I was first married to Hal, we never had a "sweet hour of prayer." We struggled! I always have been the big talker, and believe it or not, Hal was more on the quiet side. So, when it came to praying together, I just took the ball and ran with it. One thought would bleed over into another as I'd scroll down my prayer concerns. I'd cover every base and then become quiet so that Hal knew it was his turn. But I hadn't left him any room! I'd prayed for everything.

It didn't take long for us to discover the joy of praying conversationally. Just as you would in normal conversation, one of us would introduce a subject—say the children—and then each of us would chime in, leaving our burdens and requests before the Lord about the kids. When we'd covered this topic, we'd go on to another subject.... When we were through, we felt so satisfied. I hadn't hogged all the time and run every base; it wasn't a competition. Now it was teamwork, and we were both winning in prayer.[4]

Then cancer struck Hal, and their prayer times together intensified. They trusted God for healing as he underwent chemotherapy. But healing didn't come. She writes:

I'd be working at the kitchen sink, watching my husband on the patio.... Hal's physical body was wasting away. At the same time, however, I was watching his spirit growing stronger through prayer—especially our prayer times together. He was becoming Exhibit A for 2 Corinthians 4:16 (KJV), "though our outward man perish, yet the inward man is renewed day by day."

... Hal died fourteen weeks after being diagnosed with cancer. But the Spirit of God was preparing Hal's soul for another realm—a realm in which prayer changed into worship and thanksgiving. I should have read the signs and realized my Hal was preparing himself for his heavenly home as I watched him on our patio—he was worshiping Jesus Christ.[5]

Even though their prayers weren't answered in the way they had hoped, Lee and Hal deepened their relationship with each other and with God through praying together. It is a treasure the enemy can never steal from her.

Stuck in a Rut?

When Dennis and Karen first began to pray together, she thought his "prayer needle" was stuck in a rut. "I could not believe my husband was praying the same Scriptures over the same list of people every single day ... after day after day," Karen wrote. "God will often add new people to his list, but some have remained on it for years and will stay on it until the Lord tells him otherwise. If you are on his list, you will be prayed for tenaciously and with consistent predictability.

"... Dennis even dictates into a pocket tape recorder the verses and burdens on his hearts for his listees. His recorder is a reminder to pray throughout the day; it also provides a vehicle for recording special insight from the Lord," Karen adds.[6]

Judy and Jerry are a praying couple who travel a great deal as intercessors for key ministries in the United States and Israel. Yet Jerry routinely prays certain Scriptures aloud each morning. He's memorized entire chapters, which he personalizes for his wife, children, and grandchildren. Psalm 91—the "Prayer of Protection"—is one he prays daily. Judy then adds her own Scripture prayers. Their prayer time is anything but dull, as I (Quin) personally can attest.

Guidelines for Couples Who Pray Together

Authors David and Jan Stoop share these suggestions—compiled from questionnaires filled out by couples who attended their seminars—for couples who want to begin praying together:

1. Take the time needed to talk with each other about your thoughts and feelings about praying together.... Talk about your expectations up front, so they don't undermine you later on.

2. Pick a specific time and make a commitment to each other at that time.

3. Don't be upset if you miss a day ... just start again the next day. Consistency will come over time.

4. Decide who will do what. For example, who decides where you will pray together? Who reminds the other that it is time to pray?... It was interesting to note that for the couples who were successful, it was more often the husband who did the reminding.

5. Start where you are both comfortable.... If only one of you is comfortable praying out loud, then you don't start there.... If one of you insists that you pray together silently, then both can be comfortable at that place and that's where you begin.

6. Set a time limit. Start small and grow from there. Anyone can pattern five or ten minutes into his or her life, as opposed to one hour. Don't try to take too much time as you begin.

7. Agree at the beginning that neither one of you will preach in your praying. A common fear is that one's spouse will use the time to preach rather than to pray.

8. Start with a list of things you want to pray about. This could
    be done individually or together. Then pray individually
    about your time of prayer before you actually come together
    for prayer.[7]

The benefits of praying with your spouse are far greater
than any problems you struggle to overcome to make it a hall-
mark of your marriage. We encourage you to seek God's direction until you find a format that works for your situation.

In the next chapter, we'll focus on important prayer principles that will help you to strengthen the effectiveness of your
prayer partnerships.

Chapter Four

Learning Prayer Principles

Pray at all times and on every occasion in the power of the Holy Spirit. Stay alert and be persistent in your prayers for all Christians everywhere.... I urge you, first of all, to pray for all people. As you make your requests, plead for God's mercy upon them, and give thanks.

EPHESIANS 6:18; 1 TIMOTHY 2:1, NLT

Scripture has much to say about prayer. But it also teaches us about our relationships with others. In the New Testament we find more than fifty "one anothers"—principles that prayer partners can apply to their own situations. Actually, they are reciprocal commands for believers. Here are but a few:

- Pray for one another ... James 5:16.
- Love one another ... John 13:34-35; Romans 13:8; 1 John 3:23.
- Accept one another ... Romans 15:7.
- Be hospitable to one another ... 1 Peter 4:9.
- Be kind to one another ... 1 Thessalonians 5:15.
- Serve one another in love ... Galatians 5:13.
- Agree with one another ... 1 Corinthians 1:10.

- Confess your sins to one another ... James 5:16.
- Forgive one another ... Ephesians 4:32; Colossians 3:13.
- Stop passing judgment on one another ... Romans 14:13.
- Teach and admonish one another ... Colossians 3:16.
- Honor one another ... Romans 12:10.
- Encourage one another ... 1 Thessalonians 5:11; Hebrews 10:25.[1]

These ideas from Scripture could well serve as foundation stones for you and your prayer partner. Team pray-ers who experience the most effective results are those who also observe such important principles as perseverance, transparency, integrity, confidentiality, humility, forgiveness, unity, and sacrifice. The following stories highlight some of these issues and also challenge us to abide by such standards.

Transparency Is Powerful

Maureen, a New York pastor's wife, organized a group of committed intercessors in her church to meet weekly to pray. Members of the Prayer Band often asked for prayer for members of the congregation they knew who seemingly had fallen away from the Lord. The group would pray, and sure enough, the following Sunday that person would be back in church. They saw many such answers to prayer.

"I knew my two older teenage sons were far from the Lord," Maureen said, "but my husband and I thought this was just a phase in their development and that it would pass. Then one day I came across this verse in my Bible reading: 'Christ is faithful as a son over God's house. And we are his house' (Heb 3:6). As I pondered what it means to 'house' the presence of God, the Lord spoke another verse to my heart: 'My house will be a house of prayer, but you have made it a den of robbers' (Lk 19:46).

"I responded by saying, 'Who? Me, Lord? I'm in charge of the Prayer Band. I'm always praying.' But the Lord corrected me. 'You are saying prayers for your sons, but you're not really *praying* for them,' He said. 'You're trying to put out a nuclear war with a BB gun. You need to fast and pray.'"

Maureen admitted to herself and to the Lord that she wasn't praying for her sons with true faith, because she doubted that God could change them. Somehow she felt unworthy to expect such an answer to prayer for her own children.

"Then I had a startling revelation," she said. "I realized faith is not a fruit of the Spirit. I couldn't work it up; I couldn't pray louder to get it or pretend I had it while I prayed. No, faith was a gift from God, and I had to depend on Him to give it to me."

Maureen asked God for faith that day—faith to fast and pray for her sons and to believe that God would change them. And the Lord answered her prayer.

"I stopped nagging my two older boys and feeling guilty about their behavior and began simply praying in faith," she said. "I didn't pray nice, motherly prayers, though. I prayed warfare prayers—pulling down strongholds of rebellion, pride, and manipulation."[2]

The Holy Spirit showed Maureen that her oldest son was dealing drugs, her middle son was involved in gang activity, and her youngest son was about to follow in their footsteps. She knew she had to be transparent and vulnerable with the Prayer Band to enlist their support in prayer.

"I went to these people I trusted and shared what the Holy Spirit had revealed to me," she said. "I drew a diagram of a target on the chalkboard in the room where the Prayer Band met and wrote my sons' names in the middle of the bull's-eye. Week after week we prayed in agreement, targeting those boys with fervent intercession."

Six months after this prayer strategy began, the breakthrough came. Maureen's two older sons yielded their lives to the Lord within two days of each other. Their turnaround had such an impact on their younger brother that he did not follow them into rebellion.

"My oldest son, who is now married, has been our youth pastor for three years," Maureen told us. "Literally hundreds and hundreds of kids have been transformed by the gospel in this youth group. My middle son heads up our drama team, and he and his wife are preparing for the mission field. My youngest, who still lives at home, has been transformed by God's power through prayer. But it only came when I yielded to the Holy Spirit and became transparent with my friends in the Prayer Band."

Maureen's story reminded us that in the Old Testament the word for *intercessor* or *intercession* is a root word in Hebrew, *paga*, which means "to fall upon, to light upon, to assail ... to meet on behalf of another ... to make peace with."[3]

"At times it seems the process [of intercession] is hit and miss, as though we have to land or 'light upon' the situation correctly 'by chance,'" says Pastor Dutch Sheets. "It isn't really hit and miss because what is by chance for us is not to our Helper, the Holy Spirit. In fact, *paga* also means 'bull's eye.' They still use this word in Israel today. When we allow Him to intercede through us ... He will cause our prayers to light upon (*paga*) the right person or place, in the right way, at the right time, bringing forth the will of God in situations."[4]

When a modern Israeli soldier hits the target in shooting practice, he shouts, "*Paga!*"—in the same way we would say, "Bull's-eye!" Through focused prayer we can "hit the bull's-eye" to assail the enemy and, on behalf of the people for whom we're interceding, trust that they will make peace with God and the people around them.

That is exactly what the intercession of Maureen and the Prayer Band achieved in the lives of her rebellious sons.

Confidentiality Is Essential

Teresa told us that a close friend she worked with fifteen years ago taught her how to pray and also became her prayer partner. Now that they live in separate states they still pray for each other. "She just knows by the Holy Spirit when I'm in desperate need of prayer and will write or call," Teresa said.

Then she and another young mother began praying together every weekday morning for just five minutes after they saw their kids off for school. "Although we still call each other for prayer regularly, we stopped praying together daily when she started working outside the home," Teresa said. "But I asked the Lord about a prayer partner to take her place—someone

I could pray with almost every day. The person's name that kept coming to mind was our pastor's wife, Leah. It seemed almost presumptuous to ask her, but I finally did, and she said she'd pray about it."

Teresa knew if her pastor's wife became her prayer partner, the matter of confidentiality would be extremely important. Leah also took the matter seriously, knowing if she agreed to become Teresa's prayer partner she would have to allow time in her schedule to honor the commitment. She prayed about it for several months before calling Teresa to say she would accept.

"We began by trying to touch base daily," Teresa said. "The five minutes sometimes went to half an hour or more, and our friendship blossomed. Today we have a deep, rich relationship. We trust each other and keep the highest level of confidences between ourselves and the throne of God. Of course, confidentiality is the key to any good prayer partnership, but it is especially critical when praying with someone in leadership."

Intercession Spares a Leader

Mary's experience with her prayer partner Gayle illustrates the sensitive nature of information shared during prayer times. For years Gayle's husband, Gerard, had been a closet drinker. The problem grew worse and was straining their marriage, but out of fear Gayle carried the burden alone for a long time. The fact that Gerard was pastor of a large church and a popular leader among other pastors complicated the matter. Public exposure would mean his removal from ministry and leadership. Several times Gayle had confronted him about her concerns, only to collide with a wall of denial.

"We had been prayer partners for about seven years when she finally confided in me about the problem, feeling I could be trusted to pray and not to talk," Mary reported. "Since I wasn't a member of their church, I could be more objective about the matter. I began praying for Gerard in my private prayer time, as well as when Gayle and I could get together or pray on the phone. Then she called to say the situation had reached a crisis level."

One evening a member of the youth prayer group in the church had seen Gerard, with a package in his hand, coming out of a liquor store on the outskirts of town. The woman in charge of youth prayer ministry had challenged the young people to pray specifically for leaders in the church. The young man, shaken by what he had seen, reported the incident to this staff member. "The first thing we do is pray," she told him. "Please don't share this with anyone else," and he agreed.

The prayer group leader called Gayle, who was out of town due to a death in her family. Gayle called Mary. They prayed together on the phone, asking God to speak directly to Gerard and to give clear guidance to everyone involved in the situation. The minute Mary hung up the phone, she fell to her knees, asking God to extend His mercy to Gerard. "Lord, have mercy and spare him," she cried. "Don't let him fall. Please, Lord, deal with him privately in such a way that he will humble himself before You. Open his ears to hear Your voice."

As she prayed and did spiritual warfare, Mary saw—in the spirit realm—a vision of Gerard walking on a high cliff, headed for the edge. As he came dangerously close, she saw two rows of men and women walking back and forth in opposite directions between Gerard and the edge of the cliff. If a gap was left between individuals in the row going one direction, those walking in the opposite direction would cover that gap. Their walking pattern prevented Gerard from going over the edge.

"The people in that vision were intercessors," Mary said. "Men and women of all kinds, shapes, and sizes who had been praying for this man, though they knew nothing of the circumstances."

After praying over the matter, the youth prayer group leader mentioned the incident in a staff prayer meeting but did not divulge the individual's identity. "At this point we don't need to know who it is—we simply need to pray," she told the church staff. "Maybe God allowed this so the person can seek God's help without suffering public exposure."

That's exactly what happened. Gayle didn't want to confront her husband over the telephone, so she said nothing about it in their conversations. Through the working of the Holy Spirit, Gerard became so convicted about his behavior that he went to a trusted friend and asked for prayer. By the time Gayle returned from her trip, Gerard admitted to his wife that he had been wrong and promised her that he had changed. Over the following weeks and months his attitude and behavior proved it to be true.

"I'm convinced that God allowed the crisis to come in the way it did because of prayer," Mary said. "It could have led to great heartache and destruction. But because people prayed instead of taking matters into their own hands, God redeemed the situation."

Humility and Forgiveness Heal Broken Relationships

Kathy Deering, our editor for this book, shares the story of how God put her together with a woman thirty-four years her senior to become her prayer partner. Beth was a mature, gifted Bible teacher, and Kathy a twenty-one-year-old newlywed and member of Beth's Bible study group. They became fast friends, partly because of Kathy's hunger to learn more about the truths of Scripture. Kathy had not grown up in a Christian home, so Beth was like a spiritual mom and mentor to her. Their praying together was a natural outgrowth of their friendship.

"I went to her house at least once a week and we would chat awhile," Kathy said, "but primarily we prayed. Sometimes we read and discussed books. We experimented with ways of hearing from God, and sometimes included others in our circle of two. With my husband, we led an evening prayer meeting at our church. We saw some prayers answered, and we encouraged each other to faithfulness when life's struggles became fierce."

Beth was an artist with her own watercolor studio, and sketching and painting were of special interest to Kathy. Since her job gave her flextime and she didn't yet have children, Kathy was able to take one afternoon a week to paint and pray with Beth.

They prayed for the salvation of family members, for friends' physical healing, for each other's marriages and children, for protection on trips, for their respective churches, for wisdom, and for each other for inner healing as need arose. "Often we heard from God when we were quiet before Him together," Kathy said. "Beth bestowed on my husband and me parental blessings we had never received through our non-Christian families of origin. It was a true partnership."

But it wasn't always smooth sailing. Their relationship was disrupted for more than a decade when they had a serious disagreement. It's a painful reality that such problems sometimes arise between the closest friends and prayer partners. The conflict had to do with a third party who asked them for prayer and personal ministry. The woman was emotionally disturbed and had many bondages in her life. Trying to minister to her became very intense and draining, and her demands began to cause tremendous chaos in Kathy's home.

"When we prayed about it, my husband and I felt this person's needs were too great for us to handle, and that we shouldn't continue trying to minister to her," Kathy said. Beth, however, felt we should continue trying to help her. She made me feel unspiritual for taking the position I did. By this time I was busy raising four kids, and Beth and I just went our separate ways."

How to resolve such a problem?

"I finally felt I should make things right," Kathy reported. "I went to Beth and apologized for hurting her, and asked her to forgive me. She was very gracious, and we began praying together again. When my kids were in school we started meeting every week, and in later years we met intermittently. She died on New Year's Eve 1999 at the age of eighty-three.

"I miss her with quiet gratitude. One day early in our friendship, the Lord told us, 'I want your lives to grow together like two gently intertwining vines.' Beth had learned the art of Ukrainian egg painting, and she created an egg for me, covered with intertwining vines. I keep it as a warm memento of a rare friendship, bathed in prayer. A more important reminder of our partnership is the maturity of my character and the nature of my prayer life after twenty-eight years of this dear woman's influence upon me."

Preventive Prayers

God is training an army to persevere in prayer. It's easy to sigh and say, "I'm tired of praying the same old prayers." God's best is to align our prayers with what the Holy Spirit wants prayed, because He knows what lies ahead of us in the way of trials.

My (Quin's) longtime prayer partner, Fran, decided about a year ago she was tired of praying what she called "catch-up" prayers after going through one crisis situation after another. So she began "preventive praying" and shared her strategy with her prayer partners.

"I'm learning to ask the Holy Spirit how to pray in advance to prevent some of these calamities," she told me as we sat on her porch talking. Just a week earlier, at the nudging of the Holy Spirit, she'd prayed that her husband Mike, a quadriplegic, would not get an infection. She had no clue as to why she had prayed that.

Then they had to make an emergency run to the hospital due to some unexplained pain Mike was experiencing. Stones in the bladder was the diagnosis. It so happened the doctor had on hand exactly the equipment needed to do laser surgery—he'd ordered it earlier for another patient but hadn't used it. Fran's "preventive prayer" paid off, as the surgery was done without delay.

She took Mike home to recuperate with a catheter installed. I was there during his days of total bed confinement and continued praying with Fran against infection or complications. Several times, as the catheter clogged, then leaked badly, it appeared we might have to rush him back to the hospital. But God answered our prayers.

"We must have confidence that God answers prayer, but we can't give Him a timetable or demand He answer in our way," Fran says. "As we pray with patience and perseverance, our character is hammered out."

Fran keeps in touch with her long-distance prayer partners by daily e-mail. She and her close friend Sally pray together regularly by phone and occasionally at a restaurant where they meet for breakfast to pray for their families. Each Tuesday morning Fran meets with seven other women as they pray for their schools, community issues, and elections. But this group's key focus is Israel—praying for God to accomplish His will in that land, and for the Jews to emigrate from Russia to Israel while the doors are still open.

Fran, who never had children of her own, has begun crying out in prayer for children lately. Recently, while waiting for Mike's surgery at the outpatient clinic, she saw a television news item about a ten-year-old in a nearby city being abducted. A man had grabbed Jessica after she got off the school bus with her two sisters.

"Earnestly, over the next few days, I prayed for Jessica, crying out for her safety and praying the kidnapper would have mercy," she told me. "Three days later the child was released— something even the newspaper said seldom happens. I praise God for alerting me so I could participate in that prayer effort."

Fran and Mike are more confined than most couples their age, but she says she doesn't feel "shut in" as many folks would. "The Lord gives us the world to pray for, and I take the assignment seriously," she said. "Even when I feel called upon to pray outside my field of influence, I know my prayers are joined with the prayers of other believers around the globe."

Prayer Keys We've Found Helpful and Effective

- *Be specific.* Jesus told a parable about a man who wakes his friend at midnight to ask for bread—specifically three loaves—for his unexpected company (see Lk 11:5).

- *Be persistent.* The man knocks continuously until his friend answers his request. This parable is not saying that prayers are needed to overcome God's reluctance to answer. Rather, it encourages us to be bold and persistent when we pray. Jesus said to ask, seek, and knock—a continuous asking, seeking, knocking (see Lk 11:8-10). This is why some prayer partners will seem to be praying the same thing over and over until victory comes—they are building their faith with persistent prayer, reminding God of His promises.

- *Be in agreement.* Jesus gave a pattern for prayers of agreement as we've already discussed (see Mt 18:19). Your prayers may seem more effective as you pray in unity with one or more partners for healing, for protection, for provision, for intervention, for deliverance, or for any other situation.

- *Be open to the Holy Spirit.* Jesus, after He ascended to heaven, sent the Holy Spirit to help us pray what is on God's heart. Whatever your circumstances or crisis, invite Him to give you insights on how to pray through. Don't be surprised if you find yourself praying things you had never "thought of" before. Those are no doubt Holy Spirit-inspired prayers (see Rom 8:26-27).

- *Be Bible based.* As you read your Bible, you will get to know God better and understand how to pray more in accordance with His will. It's not unusual for intercessors to have a Bible verse seem to "leap off the page" at them as God's promise for the situation they are praying about. In reading and studying the Bible, you will discover more about what the Lord has to say about salvation, healing, family values, deliverance, life on earth, and heaven's promises. In other words, you will be better equipped to pray.

- *Be willing to fast.* Serious pray-ers often combine fasting with their prayer time, voluntarily abstaining from food or television or whatever the Lord lays on their heart to give up for a specific time (see Mt 6:16-18).

- *Be thankful.* When presenting requests to God, do so with thanksgiving—thanking Him in advance for answering your prayer His way and in His timing (see Phil 4:6).

- *Be a praiser.* When we praise Him, we put ourselves in a position to receive His blessings. Our focus is on Him, not just on our need. Psalm 22 affirms God's goodness while asking for His presence. He is enthroned in the praises of His people (see Ps 22:3).

- *Be trusting of Him always.* When we come to the end of ourselves, we still praise Him. "We have no power [nor do we] know what to do, but our eyes are upon you" (2 Chr 20:12). We continue to praise God for His mercy, lovingkindness, grace, and truth.

We agree with author Tommy Tenney, who writes, "We must fix our eyes, our hearts and our hopes on the King of glory and offer Him sacrifices of praise and worship. As we labor together to enthrone Him upon our praises, He will come and make us one, and we will have answered the heart's desire of God Himself."[5]

Chapter Five

Faith Building 101

Without faith it is impossible to please God, because anyone who comes to him must believe that he exists and that he rewards those who earnestly seek him.... This is the victory that has overcome the world, even our faith.

HEBREWS 11:6; 1 JOHN 5:4b

Intercession goes hand in hand with other spiritual gifts, including the gift of faith. During intercession all our spiritual gifts—from the gift of mercy to the gift of prophecy—may come into play.

In prayer-partner situations, the different gifts of the participants complement one another. Where I lack faith or experience or giftedness, my prayer partners will have what is needed. And my gifts can make up for what they lack. This is the body of Christ in action. Of course our faith must always be based on the Word of God. But our faith can be markedly increased simply by praying in concert with others.

Faith Overcomes Obstacles

I (Ruthanne) had an experience with my prayer partner, Cindy, that strengthened the faith of both of us. For years she had prayed for me as I traveled on numerous missions trips with my husband. Then one day I felt the Lord leading me to ask her to come along on my next trip to Haiti. I was taking a team of workers for a week of ministry at an orphanage near Port-au-Prince, founded by my friend Eleanor Workman. Part of the outreach included conducting medical clinics in two locations, and Cindy has a degree in nursing.

"I want you to pray about going with me to Haiti," I told her the next time we prayed together on the phone.

Long silence. "That seems pretty impossible," she finally responded.

Then she told me all the reasons why it just couldn't happen. She would have to get a babysitter to stay with her two girls. Her husband would have to agree to let her go—and since he had little or no interest in missions, that was unlikely. She had no money for such a project and saw no way she could raise the funds.

"Never mind all the obstacles," I said, "will you pray in agreement with me for God to make a way? I believe the Lord prompted me to ask you to join the team, and if He wants you to go, He can do whatever is necessary to make it happen."

"OK," she agreed. "But there's not much time to work all this out." We prayed a prayer of agreement that day, and I also had my husband pray with me about it. Over the next few weeks, as we continued to pray, we saw the Lord remove all the obstacles one by one.

Members of Cindy's church heard about the Haiti outreach and began making donations toward her trip. Her daughters cleaned out their toy boxes, gathered their outgrown clothes, and had a garage sale to raise money for their mom. Her husband, who had said none of their personal funds could be used, was surprised when all the money needed came in. Then, even more amazing, he volunteered to take vacation time from his job to stay with the girls.

I put Cindy's name on the list, and we ordered her ticket. By departure time, she had all she needed to pay for air travel, hotel, and meals. She even had extra money to give her husband to pay for special treats for the girls while she was gone.

Cindy was an invaluable member of that team—and not just for her nursing skills. As the team leader I had to deal with several unexpected problems, and her wisdom and prayer support were a tremendous help. Only after we got back home did she tell me that since childhood she had had a secret wish to go on such a trip. Her desire became reality through our prayers of agreement.

"That trip to Haiti, and praying in agreement with you and Eleanor, catapulted my walk of faith to a higher level than I'd ever known before," Cindy said, looking back on the event. "When Eleanor told me, 'I believe the money will come in without a ripple on the water,' my faith soared. And just three months later, God provided the funds for a trip back to Haiti."

This story illustrates the truth of Hebrews 11:1: "Now faith is being sure of what we hope for and certain of what we do not see." Obviously, the things we hope for must align with God's will for us. But praying with prayer partners often emboldens us to take a step of faith.

Living by Faith, Not by Sight

Have you ever asked God for a sign that a spiritual break-through was coming in a situation you'd prayed about for years? Or at least some indication that He has heard and is working? God did this for Maria through some unusual events.

Maria raised her children to adulthood as a single mom, then sold her home and lived in various locations. But she was always praying for one daughter, Candace, who had moved to Oregon and chosen to remain estranged from her for almost two decades. When they first married, Candace and her husband had lived close to Maria, and the three of them prayed together regularly. Then Chuck got involved with a cultlike group and began to control his wife's every move and alienate her from her mom.

Four years ago, while living on the East Coast, Maria visited a friend's home Bible study just at the time she'd been asking God for a sign that He was working on her behalf. As she headed down the stairs to the meeting room she was amazed when Ned, an acquaintance she had not seen for twenty years, recognized her and greeted her.

"How is your daughter?" he asked.

His question startled Maria. "Candace has been brain-washed by a controlling, demanding husband, who quotes Scripture to keep her in submission," she responded. "He often abuses her, and sometimes has kept her a virtual prisoner in her own home, except for when she's at work. I'm not allowed to see my two grandchildren—not even to write or call them."

Maria told Ned how Candace once took refuge at an abuse shelter because Chuck had beaten her. When counselors advised her to find a "safe house" for at least six months, she and the children came to stay with Maria. But soon Candace went back to Chuck and became the family's breadwinner again.

At least once a year Maria would fly to the West Coast, hoping to see her grandchildren. When she was refused, friends often joined her for a "prayer drive" around their home. But Maria never has stopped praying for the family's total restoration.

After bringing Ned up-to-date on Candace, Maria took a seat beside a woman in a two-person pew. Ned, it turned out, was the leader of the Bible study. He introduced Maria and said, "I think she needs to tell our group what she's just told me about her daughter so we can pray for this situation."

Maria had been amazed to see Ned at this meeting, and now was astonished that he'd ask these believers to pray for her daughter. But soon she got another surprise—a confirmation that God was indeed concerned about her problems. After briefly sharing her story with the group, she sat down.

"I've heard that story before, but I've never met you," the woman sharing the pew told her, obviously puzzled.

"Maybe you read it in the book *A Woman's Guide to Breaking Bondages*," Maria answered. "I shared it with my friend Quin Sherrer, one of the authors, and she put it in the book."[1]

"Yes! That's it!" the woman said. "I read that book at least two years ago, and I've prayed every day for that grandmother. You mean that was you? Well, I won't stop praying."

I (Quin) had lunch with Maria recently when she was in my area. She told me about this incident, and how encouraged she was to learn a total stranger had been praying daily for her. She had a prayer partner she wasn't even aware of!

Today her grandchildren are young teenagers, and she still isn't allowed any communication with them. Her daughter has phoned her twice in all these years—but even that is a breakthrough. Another answer to prayer is that Candace sent her two photos—one of the children, and one of her and her husband. Maria lays hands on those pictures as she prays for them, confident that God will answer.

Stories of Grace From Prison

Dorothy may be a graying grandmother, but she has a powerful prison ministry. When she and one or more prayer partners go into women's prisons, amazing things happen. Two of her stories illustrate the power of God's grace, even in the most difficult of circumstances.

Accompanied by Judy, a praying friend, Dorothy was preaching at a state institution for women when she noticed an inmate sitting in the front row who kept rubbing her arm, which was wrapped in a black cloth cast. As soon as Dorothy finished, she and Judy asked the woman if they could pray for her. The prisoner agreed but quickly told them why she needed prayer for more than her hurting arm.

"I am three months pregnant, and the doctors want me to abort my baby," she said. "I have a tumor, and if it bursts, both the baby and I will die." Dorothy and Judy prayed in agreement for the woman's total healing, then told her to look to the Lord for the answer.

Several months later Dorothy was back in the main prison yard on a Thursday night and this same woman was waiting to talk to her. "I'm the one who had the tumor and the baby," she said. "I wanted to tell you the tumor has disappeared, and the baby is just fine. My broken arm is healed, too."

Naturally, Dorothy and Judy were happy to hear that report. Prison officials had released her from prison for the baby's birth, and her little girl was born on Thanksgiving Day. She named her Grace, acknowledging that she had received grace from God Himself.

On another occasion when Dorothy and two prayer partners were ministering in the main prison yard, a young woman we'll call Heather came to ask for prayer. With sorrow etched on her face, she told them she had delivered a baby earlier that same day, but the baby had died. "Lord, give Heather the comfort and peace that only You, the Creator God, can give," Dorothy's partners prayed as the tearful woman stood before them. "Let her know You have her little one in Your tender care. Holy Spirit, please let Your presence comfort her grieving heart."

A year later Heather was back in chapel again, asking for prayer. "I have cancer of the cervix, and doctors are to operate on me next Monday," she said, even more distraught than she had been over her baby's death.

Dorothy and her partners prayed a simple, faith-packed prayer. "Heather, I believe if we pray in agreement down here, God hears us up there and He answers," Dorothy said.

On Monday, when the woman checked into the hospital for the operation, doctors could find no cancer. The chaplain called Dorothy immediately to give her the good news. She and the women who have gone faithfully for years to bring hope and faith to these women behind bars rejoiced and thanked God for yet another miracle.

Most of us probably can't go into a prison to pray for someone we don't know. But we can pray for those who are in the path God has set for us—and choose a prayer partner to agree with us, too!

Prayers for a Troubled Prisoner

Vivian and Dan, another couple who minister to women in prison, often face the frustration of having prisoners suddenly transferred without warning. They have no way of finding out why they were moved, or of tracking them through the system.

One woman we'll call Helen had rededicated her life to the Lord in one of their meetings and begun attending regularly— even participating by occasionally giving her testimony. Then she started skipping meetings. One of the last times she came, Dan warned her that she was wavering from one side to the other, and he urged her to totally commit her life to Christ. She came once more, then stopped.

They sent her cards and letters, but got no response. Then someone told them that Helen was in a lesbian relationship. Vivian and Dan continued praying in agreement that Helen would turn back to the Lord. The following year they visited a correctional facility in another city more than one hundred miles away where God had just opened a door for them to minister.

"When we got to the meeting room, Helen was the first one

there!" Vivian told us. "She had been transferred to this place several months before. She thanked us for the cards and letters, and all our prayers for her, and said she felt it in her heart each time we prayed. She again committed her life to the Lord and is trying to truly follow Him. We praised God all the way home for bringing Helen back to Jesus."

"Adopted" Prayer Partners

When you are far from home and facing a medical crisis, how desperately you need prayer partners to uphold you. This was Billy and Susan's situation when they traveled from Florida to Houston for his cancer treatments. They had no idea it would end up a two-year ordeal. Nor did they realize how much they'd miss the hands-on caring of their own praying church, where they'd been members for over thirty years.

One Sunday while in Houston they visited a small church. In the bulletin was a notice that those needing special prayer could come to the altar after the service for prayer. They made their way to the front, where a team of pray-ers met them and began to intercede. On learning of the seriousness of Billy's condition, one couple "adopted" them as a long-term prayer project.

Billy underwent eight surgeries during those two years, eventually having his right arm amputated to save his life. Every Sunday the entire congregation prayed for him. At least once a week a man from that church came to encourage him, to pray with him, and just to let him talk.

Someone was always there to pray with Susan while her husband was undergoing surgery. These new friends, who joined her in prayer as they wrestled for Billy's very life, helped sustain her. She believes God led them to this church—after they had visited others—giving them a church home away from home.

Now, three years later, Billy returns to Houston for a checkup every six months. Friends there still keep up with him and Susan and continue to pray for his well-being.

A Word From God Builds Faith

We're all aware that even when you have raised children in a Christian home, they may choose not to follow the faith of their parents. Doris and Ben faithfully took their children to church and lived a Christian life before them. Their two daughters grew up loving the Lord and never strayed. But their son, Bob, married a girl whose parents were not Christians and she had no desire to become one. Bob followed in her footsteps.

For thirty years Doris and Ben have prayed together faithfully for their prodigal son. Because Bob and his family live outside the U.S., they don't see them often. Saddened because their grandchildren are not in church, Doris and Ben visit when they can and take the kids to church in the town where they live.

"God spoke to me and assured me that Bob will come into the kingdom," Doris told me (Quin). "I know God's voice and I'm trusting in Him. Lois, our daughter-in-law, called us once and said her cousin led her to the Lord and that she was very happy. But I never saw any indication that she'd followed

through with it. We bought her a Bible, but there was no growing in the Lord, and no church attendance."

Day after day Doris prays from Acts 26:18, personalizing the
verse for their daughter-in-law: "God, open Lois' eyes and turn
her from darkness to light, from the power of Satan, unto
God, that she may receive forgiveness of sins, and an inheri-
tance among those who are sanctified by faith in Christ."

Only one of their grandchildren is a Christian, but that
means Doris and Ben pray all the more for the others. When
I (Quin) visited their home recently, I joined their daily prayer
time as they committed all their children and grandchildren
to our heavenly Father's care.

Some Prayers Answered Gradually

One mom who prayed for years for God to protect the marriages of her children grew increasingly concerned about one
of her sons, Neil. She wrote us about her prayer solution:

My son was staying away from church and making poor
choices for his life and marriage. On the other hand, my
daughter-in-law, Pat, was moving closer to the Lord. As I
encouraged her, there came a day when we both felt a
strong commitment to pray together. We began meeting
on Tuesday evenings, and soon it became clear that my
son was our focal point of prayer. We have prayed faithfully week after week, month after month.

Sometimes when Pat is too discouraged or angry with
Neil to pray aloud, I ask her to agree in silence while I

pray. We've grown closer through our prayer times and more confident as we cover my two grandsons with God's protection. One day we both sensed things were changing and were encouraged when Neil attended a men's retreat at our church and had a "breaking" experience while there. I wish I could say he has turned around entirely, but there is still a long road to go.

Good progress has been made, though. And Pat and I both believe that God will "tip over our bowl of prayers" in His season. Meanwhile, we thank Him for the miracle of our relationship, for His protection over this marriage, and for the children who are growing in His love.

We share a story about a family that has not seen total victory just to let you know that not all families experience instant triumph. Don't be surprised if your prayers are answered gradually—not immediately. But any sign of progress is a confirmation that prayer is paying off. Besides, it spurs us on to keep praying, believing, and stretching our faith—based on God's promises to us.

Of course, we do experience seemingly sudden answers to prayer on occasion. The next story illustrates the power of a husband and wife praying in agreement.

Prayer of Agreement Brings Reconciliation

At a Mother's Day tea where I (Quin) was speaking, Barbara and her twenty-two-year-old daughter, Lisa, came to share with me what they considered a miracle of reconciliation, all because of prayer. Barbara and her husband had been ~ about Lisa, who wouldn't let them speak of God in her presence without making a negative or derogatory comment. What's more, she didn't come home much.

Barbara read our book *A Woman's Guide to Spiritual Warfare* and began to pray a suggested prayer for children she'd found in the book, personalizing it for Lisa. She did this for two weeks without seeing any improvement. Then she had an idea:

"I asked my husband, Don, to agree with me by reading this prayer during our prayer time together," Barbara said. "Within two more weeks our daughter went to the altar at church, and a transformation began in her that has been awesome. Whereas once she couldn't stand to come home, now she doesn't want to leave. Before this, my husband and I dreaded her coming home because she brought such turmoil. Now our home is peaceful and we look forward to our times together. God is faithful when we agree in prayer.

"Your books confirm to me over and over what the Holy Spirit has taught me in learning to battle spiritual darkness. Our unconditional love for one another brings us into unity with God in an unstoppable wave of power. If only we could tap into an understanding of this power, we as a church body would never cease praying." (See appendix for the prayer she prayed.)

Triplets of Prayer

When Evelyn Christenson, well-known author on prayer, had a desire to see people come to faith in Jesus throughout the world, she established what she calls "triplet praying." Three

Christians choose three unsaved people (making a total of nine) to pray for. These three get together once a week for a minimum of fifteen minutes to pray exclusively for those nine individuals, especially for their salvation.

As the triplet movement has swept around the world, many have been won to Christ. It was Evelyn's longtime dream to see entire communities and nations filled with triplets of praying Christians. In her book *A Time to Pray*, she gives additional examples of this type of prayer.

"Three together, triplets of people, are common in the Bible," she writes. "Jesus had His inner circle of three—Peter, James, and John. They were the ones with Him in some of His most intimate times.... But most important is Jesus' wonderful promise that when two or three Christians gather together in His name, He is in their midst."[2]

All of us need support teams—people we can count on to pray for us. But we can also join support teams, as Evelyn suggests, to pray for other people's needs.

Building a Church Through Prayer Teams

One winter morning Pastor Phil was driving near his city in New York state when he noticed a huge building for sale. Suddenly he felt God was saying he should take steps toward purchasing this property. His congregation of about 350 already owned a beautiful, paid-for building, so the idea seemed far-fetched. After he prayed for divine confirmation, three visiting ministers soon confirmed that indeed God wanted the church to expand its impact on the community.

Pastor Phil then shared the matter with the congregation, and asked them to form forty prayer triplets, making a total of 120 intercessors. Soon prayer teams were meeting to pray at least once a week—in homes, at lunchtime, over the phone, and in the parking lot of the building.

Through the sales agent, the owner said, "This piece of real estate is too expensive for God!" That spurred the prayer teams to prayerwalk around the empty building seven times, ending with a shout of victory. When Pastor Phil spoke directly to the owner, the man scoffed at the idea of a church buying his property. So the prayer teams focused on praying that God would soften his heart, even that he would have sleepless nights and think about what God was doing.

After five months a different property owner called one day, saying he wanted to share a "God experience." While driving near the same property being prayed over, he felt God said to him, "Pastor Phil needs your land"—a forty-eight-acre tract directly across the highway from the building for sale. Large corporations had already made offers on the land, but no deals had been closed. "My partners and I are willing to sell this land to the church for half our former asking price," the man said.

Here was a better price, no extensive renovations needed, and they could design their own building. A few days later when the pastor stopped his car to pray outside the gate of this man's huge estate, the gentleman came walking down the driveway to get his mail. Upon seeing who was in the car he began railing at Pastor Phil, claiming he'd caused him many sleepless nights. "Leave this property and never return," the man ordered.

Clearly, God was giving direction through the owner's response! The prayer teams now began praying over negotiations on the forty-eight-acre tract of land, and for God's direction concerning disposition of their current building. Then the pastor learned that the local library was looking for a new location, and their church property fit all the criteria of the library search committee.

"The prayer teams have played an integral part in this process," Pastor Phil reported. "Now that we have a binding contract, the teams continue to pray—often on the property itself—for the needed funds to complete the project. God has given us great favor not only with the owners, but with city officials we must deal with to get permits of all kinds. It is stretching the faith of all of us, but God is definitely at work here."

Mary, one of the intercessors involved in this massive effort, told us, "My team was formed of church members I really trust who live close to me. Not only have we seen prayers answered, but praying together has caused a strong bond of love and unity between us. I can't believe I went so many years without prayer partners."

We see a scriptural example of a triplet support team in the story of Moses, Aaron, and Hur in Exodus 17:8-13. Moses, Israel's leader, stood on a hill overlooking the valley where his troops were fighting an invading army. As long as he held up his hands with his staff stretched out over the valley, Israel was winning. But when weariness caused his hands to droop, the enemy began to gain the upper hand. Aaron and Hur stood on either side of Moses and held up his hands until sunset; thus Israel won the victory.

It's been our experience that when we are willing to hold up the weary hands of a fellow believer, God always provides intercessors to stand by us when we're needing prayer support. And all of us have our faith strengthened.

Chapter Six

Praying With Vision and Expectation

I urge, then, ... that requests, prayers, intercession and thanksgiving be made for everyone.... This is good, and pleases God our Savior, who wants all men to be saved and to come to a knowledge of the truth.

1 TIMOTHY 2:1, 3-4

Vision and expectation are essential elements if prayers of agreement are to be successful. As we see in the next story, a crisis can become a catalyst for bonding people together in prayer for a shared concern.

When the fourth elderly person in a quiet Southern college town was murdered in their own neighborhood, Connie and her husband, Richard, agreed something had to be done. As staunch believers, they knew their area needed to be watched over not only by local residents but primarily by God and His host of angels.

With the approval of both the sheriff's department and the city council, Connie and Richard set up a Neighborhood Watch. Going door to door with flyers, they invited people from ninety homes near them to attend the initial meeting. Then eight block captains were appointed—most of them Christians.

For nearly three years now the neighbors have become closer to one another, watching out for strangers or suspicious activity. And many block captains lead their groups in prayer for the neighborhood. Residents are sprucing up the neighborhood, and a park is being renovated. Children are playing in the yards again. Young married couples are buying and refurbishing some of the older houses once rented to college students—who often spent their evenings sitting on the porches smoking marijuana.

Some of the women Connie met through the Neighborhood Watch have become her close prayer partners. "What the enemy meant for evil in our neighborhood, God has turned for the good," she reported. "I now have a new prayer partner, and we pray together daily on the phone and twice a week in person. Our primary prayer target is the abused children in our city."

After the Neighborhood Watch began, one more murder was committed in another part of town, but no more have occurred. None of the five cases have been solved. In fact, while we were writing this book, a national television network highlighted the city's distress over the mysterious killings. Even that didn't lead to any arrests. Connie and Richard continue to pray the murders will be solved, but meanwhile, they're grateful for God's protection over their town.

"Many neighborhoods across our nation have block parties at least once a year—where neighbors gather to get to know each other better," Connie said. "But imagine the powerful results if more of them got together to pray for one another!"

We're happy to report we've actually heard of some communities where this is happening. Our friend Mary Lance Sisk has witnessed many miracles in the neighborhoods of her city since scores of women have begun prayerwalks. Some of the most outstanding results are the many small neighborhood prayer triplets formed as the movement grows.

"I believe the key to the healing of the United States is going to be neighborhood by neighborhood, with women doing it!" she says. "Evangelism is a lifestyle of love that results from having Jesus' heart for the lost."

Mary Lance encourages women to intercede daily for their neighbors and to pray for God to raise up a prayer movement in each neighborhood. She takes literally Jesus' command to "love your neighbor as yourself" and Peter's admonition to "proclaim the praises of Him who called you out of darkness into His marvelous light" (1 Pt 2:9, NKJV).

Walking on her street, she makes it a habit to proclaim Scripture. "Lord, we invite the King of Glory to come in. Come forth and bring your glory into this neighborhood. Release your blessing to the families here."[1]

A Wall of Prayer Around Our Children

More than a dozen years ago, five women in Lexington, Kentucky, read my (Quin's) first book, *How to Pray for Your Children.* Then they went on a mini-retreat to watch the video I had done on the same topic.[2]

"We saw a need to build a wall of prayer around our children, because the enemy obviously was seeking to destroy them," one of the women said. "Since we had about thirty children and grandchildren among us, we got the idea to meet regularly to pray for one another's children. We asked God to teach us how to pray, and to help us do it on a routine basis."

At first the five women met weekly in local parks and prayed for each other's children. After sharing their vision in local churches, home groups, and schools, they helped set up several "How to Pray for Your Children" groups in the city. People kept giving them praise reports of fantastic answers to prayer for their youngsters.

Before long the husbands of the original five women began to join the wives in their prayer sessions. Twelve years later all five husbands are still involved. Gathering at Dorothea and Bob's home one night a week, they begin with a covered dish supper, then share reports of answered prayer. Finally they break into small prayer circles to pray specifically for one another's children. At the end, each person takes the name of another parent's child (or children) to pray for in the coming week.

Today nineteen people are involved—including six couples, four single moms, and three husbands whose wives can't always come. Every time I go to Lexington, I meet with them and always leave excited and encouraged. Their meetings now rotate between various homes, as members want to share the blessing of hosting the group.

"Did your husbands feel uncomfortable praying aloud when they started meeting with the wives?" I asked Dorothea.

"Yes, praying aloud was a new experience for most of them," she answered. "They were a bit reluctant at first. Even uncomfortable. But now there's no hesitation among any of us to pray aloud. We see how much our kids are under attack, and we wonder where they'd be today if we hadn't been praying."[3]

Dorothea remembers how the children used to moan and groan when they knew it was the night their parents would gather to pray for them. "Now they call and ask prayer for themselves and their children—not just for our Wednesday-night prayer meeting but at other times, too," she said.

One exciting answer to prayer came a few months back when the entire prayer group went to a café in a town ten miles away for some on-site praying. The new business is operated by three children of one of the couples in the prayer group—working as manager, chef, and waitress. Since their start-up had been slow, the group of parents came to eat and to pray. Not only did they pray blessings over the children and their new business, they also prayed for the community.

Amazingly, the very next day, business picked up, and it has been booming ever since. "When other challenges face them, I'm sure we'll pray for those, too," Dorothea reported.

They have seen answered prayers on many fronts—from children coming to the Lord, to finding the right colleges (some with scholarships), jobs, mates, and careers. Some have prayed grandchildren through horrific health problems and have seen the healing hand of God move in those situations.

Over a year ago Dorothea helped a group of mothers get started in Mount Sterling, about an hour away. Eight to ten moms meet every Monday evening for one hour, just before suppertime, to pray for their offspring.

"They knew each other as friends for some time, but not until they started praying together did they really get to know and appreciate one another," Dorothea told me. "They said they have developed such a love for each others' children now that they pray for them once a week." Dorothea is their "cheerleader," constantly encouraging them by phone or in person. (See appendix for addresses of various prayer movements.)

Releasing Blessings in Your Neighborhood

When I (Quin) walk through a three-block area in our neighborhood pulling a little red wagon loaded with my grandchildren, the ordinary observer sees a grandmother taking the kids on an outing. But in reality we are on a prayerwalk.

As we go down the sidewalk we'll sing, sometimes making up verses to go with popular tunes they already know. Often all we do is sing "Hallelujah" in front of each home. I may offer a short prayer and they add their "Amen." They are learning that prayer can take place outside our home or church and that we really care for our neighbors.

Prayerwalking simply means *praying on-site* in your neighborhood *with insight* from the Holy Spirit as to how to pray. Experienced intercessors suggest these preliminary steps before beginning such an outreach in your neighborhood or city:

- Prepare your heart with the Lord.
- Evaluate your neighborhood (or city) by learning something of its history and layout. Don't take on too much territory all at once. For instance, Mary Lance suggests you might want to walk several streets in your neighborhood, but only pick one to five families to pray for on a regular basis during your devotional time.
- Ask for His purpose and vision for your prayerwalk.
- Seek God for guidance as to what Scriptures to use as you

walk. Memorize some that you can say aloud as you walk, declaring God's love for your city.[4]

"Walking helps sensitize you to the realities of your community," write Steve Hawthorne and Graham Kendrick in their book *Prayerwalking*. "Sounds, sights and smells, far from distracting your prayer, engage both body and mind in the art of praying. Better perception means boosted intercession.... Walking also connects Christians with their own neighborhoods. By regularly passing through the streets of their cities, walkers can present an easygoing accessibility to neighbors. Walking seems to create opportunities to help or to pray for new friends on the spot, right at the times of great need. Some streets present risks, but vulnerability yields valuable contact with those who have yet to follow Christ."[5]

They suggest three things a prayer intercessor must do to walk and pray for a city:

- Stand before God offering gifts of praise, especially thanks offerings.
- Stand with your city in repentance—cry for mercy (see Lk 19:41-44).
- Stand in your city, extending blessings from God's heart.[6]

Prayer Brings Revival to the County Jail

A cooperative prayer effort in a small Texas town led to revival in the local county jail. Members from two churches prayer-walked the town, distributing Christmas cards with a prayer message to every home. They considered returning the two hundred leftover cards to the supplier, when two ladies suggested sending them to prisoners and staff at the county jail. Church members signed each card personally, praying that God would touch the life of each staff member and prisoner receiving one.

They were surprised when a flood of personal thank-you notes followed—some signed by all the inmates in a cell block. After the holidays, church members prayed for the people individually, and a women's group began prayerwalking around the jail. They claimed the area for the Lord and prayed for everyone inside. Chapel attendance in the jail increased almost immediately and tripled within six months. At least seventeen inmates have made decisions for Christ and been baptized. Now the prisoners help lead the worship and prayer times. "Revival is going on at the jail, and it's because of prayer," reported one participant.[7]

Changing Your Neighborhood Through Prayer

Could our communities truly be transformed by Christ if every neighbor and neighborhood were prayed for daily? LeRoy and I (Quin) were asked to take part in answering that question one spring as Christians from numerous churches in our city pledged to pray for their neighborhoods.

The goal was for each person or couple to pray blessings over five neighbors and then to be available to them when needed. We agreed to pray:

Five blessings for
Five neighbors for
Five minutes a day
Five days a week for
Five weeks.

Each member of our congregation willing to participate took a sheet of instructions with these suggestions. Who is your neighbor? Jesus described a neighbor as someone you meet along life's road who needs your help. Think of the word BLESS to remember five important ways to pray for your neighbors:

B—*Body:* health, protection, strength
L—*Labor:* work, income, security
E—*Emotions:* joy, peace, hope
S—*Social:* love, marriage, family, friends
S—*Spiritual:* salvation, faith, grace[8]

Always pray with a clean heart. The prayers of the righteous are powerful and effective (see Jas 5:16). Pray with compassion. Be like Christ, who was moved with compassion toward the needy (see Mt 9:36). Pray with persistence (see Acts 12:5; Jas 5:17).[9]

We chose five specific neighbors to pray for during our early-morning prayer time, and we've already seen results in the lives of three of these in our subdivision.

• One couple who had been living together finally got married in a downtown church.

- A family with a cursing father and obnoxious, disobedient children finally moved away. The children caused havoc when they were all out in the yard at once—throwing rocks, pulling up flowers, and, when adults weren't looking, ganging up on other children. Peace was restored to the neighborhood when they left. The country setting to which they relocated is much more suited to their way of living, giving the children room to roam and explore.

- A bridge of communication opened with another neighbor, when a man and wife unexpectedly rang our doorbell to ask if my husband would come conduct the wedding for their son. Family and friends had anxiously waited a couple of hours, but the pastor they'd asked hadn't shown up. While my husband put on his blue suit, we prayed and asked God to help him to exalt Jesus. While some might have said, "Let them call a notary," LeRoy agreed because it gave him the opportunity to explain a Christian marriage from God's perspective. Those neighbors have certainly become friendlier—they even came to our garage sale.

We continue to pray for our other neighbors, that they will come to a saving knowledge of Christ. Once a week my husband goes out to eat with one of the men we are praying for. LeRoy's goal is to develop a trusting relationship with him, rather than hitting him on the head with the gospel. Once, before this man was to undergo serious surgery, he allowed LeRoy and me to come pray for him. That in itself was a victory.

Some plant, some water, and some bring in the harvest. We don't care which of those roles the Lord has for us; we just want to be faithful to do our part.

Ministering in the Inner City

Carl and Angie, who have planted a small church in one of the oldest and most run-down areas of their city, asked God for creative ideas for reaching that neighborhood. After they taught a series on prayer, members began prayerwalking around the church every week, asking God's peace and blessings over the families. Once a year they bake more than two hundred dozen cookies to take door-to-door. "We want you to know we're praying for you, and these cookies are for your children," they tell the residents.

Some members deliver homemade lunches to homeless people farther downtown, while others are prayerwalking the immediate neighborhood. Three mornings a week they offer free food and clothing at the church. Several homeless people and many nearby neighbors attend worship services from time to time, where they are showered with love and prayers.

"We see barriers down, and people speaking to one another and to us," Angie told us. "People used to be afraid to socialize among each other, and that is changing. Yards are being cleaned, houses painted, and flowers planted. The people always thank us for singing Christmas carols on their street and bringing them cookies. At last a government plan to replace the nearby crime-ridden public housing complex is under way."

This small congregation of only about fifty people is making a huge spiritual impact on the community. They see with their own eyes the powerful result of combining corporate prayer with practical outreach.

A Prayer Movement That Lasted One Hundred Years?

Yes! Pray-ers actually took hourly prayer watches in a movement that changed the eighteenth century. Many have marveled at the accounts of the famous Moravian community of Herrnhut in Saxony, Germany, whose members prayed for revival. They were young but hungry for God. Even the leader, Count von Zinzendorf, had not yet reached thirty.

Based on Leviticus 6:13 ("The fire must be kept burning on the altar continuously; it must not go out"), they began prayer meetings, believing the fire on the altar should be prayer. Discord and dissension plagued them the first five years, but they persisted.

On May 12, 1727, revival came. Three months later, twenty-four men and twenty-four women covenanted to spend one hour each day in scheduled prayer. Around-the-clock prayer watches—often in groups of two or three—continued nonstop for more than a hundred years.

History records that sixty-five years after they'd started that prayer vigil, the Moravian community had sent three hundred missionaries around the world. God seemed to ignite in them two passions: one for prayer and the other to reach the lost "for whom no one cared," in Zinzendorf's words. Their theme: "To win for the Lamb that was slain the rewards of His sufferings."[10]

In the centuries following the Moravians, interest in prayer declined, increased during the years of the Great Awakening, then declined again. But today we see a resurgence of emphasis on prayer worldwide.

Large prayer gatherings have taken place in cities all over the world, as well as here in the U.S. For instance, in 1997 the Promise Keepers movement called for a million men to go to Washington, D.C., to seek God's face through prayer and repentance. Speakers emphasized the need for turning the hearts of the fathers to the children (see Mal 4:5-6).

Three years later "The Call" took place, also in our nation's capital. Several hundred thousand young people and some parents gathered on the Capitol Mall to fast and pray for a great awakening among the youth of the nation. Repentance and reconciliation were prominent themes during the twelve-hour event.

Many prayer organizations are involved in what is now called the Lighthouse Movement, with lighthouses of prayer being formed in neighborhoods across the nation. Leaders of the movement define a lighthouse as "a gathering of two or more people in Jesus' name for the purpose of praying for, caring for, and sharing Christ with their neighbors and others in their sphere of influence."[11]

Global Prayer

During the last decade of the twentieth century, another prayer watch was extremely effective in praying for people in regions where the gospel has not yet had a substantial impact. Yet an even larger thrust is expected in this millennium.

"We are poised for the most massive prayer offensive into the kingdom of darkness that history has ever known," says Dr. C. Peter Wagner, who has been instrumental in spearheading the international prayer effort.[12]

First was the call to pray for the nations in the 10/40 Window—so named because of their latitude-longitude location on the globe. Now the effort includes countries in Europe, Scandinavia, the Caucasus Region, and North and Central Asia—called the 40/70 Window. While many will be praying for these nations from their own homes and churches, others will join prayer teams to travel to these locations for specific on-site praying.

Over the past few years, united prayer teams have trekked from the tropical climate of Guatemala to the mountainous slopes of Nepal. From their homelands to Romania, Egypt, Iraq ... and on and on. Once sixteen prayer-journey teams were mobilized on three continents, made up of ordinary men, women, and youth intercessors. Praying as they walked, they stood against forces of darkness to prepare the way for the gospel to be shared so that millions can come to Christ.

Truly, it is God's desire that we pray for all men to come to a knowledge of the truth concerning Jesus, our Savior. We can pray with great expectation for results, knowing we're praying according to His will.

A statement by Charles Finney, a fiery nineteenth-century evangelist who broke with tradition by allowing women to pray in public, sums up the essence of what we believe: "You need not look for an answer to prayer if you pray without any expectation of obtaining it."[13]

Chapter Seven

Distance Doesn't Matter

*A centurion came to him [Jesus], asking for help. "Lord,"
he said, "my servant lies at home paralyzed and in terrible
suffering." Jesus said to him, "I will go and heal him." The
centurion replied, "Lord, I do not deserve to have you come
under my roof. But just say the word, and my servant will
be healed."*

MATTHEW 8:5-8

Prayer partnerships can span the globe. Faith-filled prayer,
when it is in agreement with the will of God, need not be
limited by geographical proximity or even by time zones. In
fact, distance really doesn't matter.

"Since prayer is unhindered by time, distance, or language
barriers, you can join any ministry team on the earth!" writes
Jim Goll. "Your prayers can make a vital difference, especially
when you harmonize in prayer with others and carefully target
your prayers.... Teams can go constantly to sow the seed of the
gospel in the earth."[1]

When Jesus met the centurion, who was seeking healing for
his servant, He was astonished at the man's strong faith—even

declaring that He had not "found anyone in Israel with such great faith" (Mt 8:10).

Why did Jesus so highly commend this man, a gentile, who had no scriptural knowledge? Because the centurion understood this truth: *There is no distance in prayer.* The centurion presented his petition to Jesus, knowing that if Jesus came into agreement with the request, the servant would be healed. Since Jesus' authority transcends time and space, it wasn't necessary for Him to be physically present to heal the man's servant.

I (Quin) am active in a women's worldwide prayer ministry that targets specific nations and people groups to pray for during the year. So, in essence, a Christian woman in a Muslim country may join her prayers with mine as we pray for her country—though I don't even speak her language. I pray for the spread of the gospel in that land, for the people there to have supernatural encounters with God, for an outpouring of the Holy Spirit, and for spiritual blindness to be lifted.

When my daughter lived for several years in a time zone eight hours ahead of mine, we coordinated our times to pray together on the phone. But often I prayed for her in the middle of the night as her day was beginning and she was leaving for work. During the time that she lived on one side of the globe, my son and his family lived five time zones away in the opposite direction. He and I coordinated our prayer times when it was midday for me and he was just getting up. But believe me, they called home day or night if they had pressing prayer needs, regardless of time zones.

Spirit-Led Intercession

One summer in 1986 when John and I (Ruthanne) were traveling in France for a full month, I became very ill. We moved from one small town to another every few days, as John was speaking in various churches pastored by his former students. Under these circumstances I didn't try to find a doctor but asked my husband to pray.

One day, while lying on the bed in our room in a French cottage, I prayed, "Lord, please speak to Cindy and ask her to pray for me." Noticing the afternoon sunlight streaming through the window, I calculated it was midmorning back in Texas where she lives. It wasn't feasible to phone her, but I knew she was praying for us during this trip. As I drifted off to sleep I trusted the Holy Spirit to give her a prayer alert.

Upon returning home I called Cindy to tell her how sick I'd been, that I was better but still struggling with symptoms. "While you were in France, the Lord impressed me to pray specifically for your immune system," she reported. "He didn't pinpoint the problem; I simply prayed as the Holy Spirit directed."

When I went to our family doctor he put me on strong antibiotics for a kidney infection, and within a couple of weeks I was OK. It was not an instant healing. But I firmly believe Cindy's prayers for my immune system, combined with the prayers of John and other friends, carried me through until I got medical help. I gained a new appreciation for the truth that prayer isn't limited by distance, and for God's gift of a faithful prayer partner.

No Surprises With God

Jeanette experienced the power of praying over the telephone when an unexpected tragedy struck her family. One morning when she awakened a little early, she called her sister Marge just to visit. But Marge seemed apprehensive. "I awakened last night with a sense of foreboding," she told Jeanette. "I began praying for God to surround the kids with His angels."

Marge and her husband, Dale, had divorced three years earlier, and he had won custody of their two children, Brad and Angela. Although Marge had visitation rights, Dale tried in every way to limit her access to her children—such as blocking her phone calls, even from every pay phone within a several-mile radius. When she came for her court-ordered visits, he would dial 911 to call the police out. Each time the onus was on Marge to prove her innocence.

That morning on the phone Jeanette remembered she had recently bought a copy of our book *How to Pray for Your Children*. She grabbed the book and began reading to Marge every prayer and Scripture pertaining to praying for one's children.

"It seemed her spirits rose a little with each prayer we said together," Jeanette said. "The last prayer was for an adult child being manipulated, controlled, or abused by a spouse. Marge uttered a great sigh of relief as we finished our exchange on the telephone."

Less than five minutes after she'd hung up, Jeanette's phone rang. "Jeanette, please pray!" Marge said with panic in her voice. Then she reported that Brad had just called her after nine-year-old Angela had found their father unconscious in the garage—maybe dead. The boy had just dialed 911.

"Amazingly, my mind was protected from conjuring up fearful images about the event Marge had just related," Jeanette said. "I was surrounded by peace and stillness. This continued, even when I later got the news that Dale was indeed dead from carbon-monoxide poisoning. He had left the van engine running after driving into the garage and closing the door."

When Angela had found her father in the garage, she managed to keep her head and called to her brother to dial 911, then call their mom. It was as if the angels were there to shield the children from the horror and terror of it all. Even Dale's mother, who normally would have blocked Marge's access to the children, was not there for some reason. Marge was able to rush over to be with Brad and Angela at a most crucial time in their lives. She prayed and wept with them, bonding with her children in a way the Lord knew was vital to their spirits.

"There is still much for everyone to go through concerning this tragedy," Jeanette reported. "But it seems God allowed it to happen in His perfect timing. How could we doubt God's mercy, when He had prepared us ahead of time for the shocking events of that morning? Thank you for your well-thought-out and powerful prayers, which seem to say exactly what my heart is struggling to express."

The Power of Perseverance

Audrey, a vivacious, energetic woman in her seventies, was hit with a pounding headache one Sunday afternoon in April. No medication seemed to alleviate her pain. By that evening she couldn't even sit up in bed.

On Monday she was diagnosed with a bladder infection and given medication, but it didn't help. On Tuesday she was admitted to the hospital, where doctors ran several exhaustive tests. Still, they could give no definite diagnosis. They only knew that she had a severe infection of some kind.

Despite massive doses of antibiotic and antiviral medications, Audrey's condition deteriorated. Extreme pain moved into her back and lower body; her temperature and blood pressure skyrocketed. When she slipped into a semi-comatose state and began having seizures, doctors put her into a drug-induced coma to stop the seizures.

For the next five weeks machines maintained all her body functions. She had no movement of any body parts, no response to stimuli, not a moan or flicker of an eyelash. When the drugs were withdrawn, brain scans showed very little activity and the seizures recurred. Audrey was moved to a medical research hospital, where more diagnostic tests continued to show minimal brain activity.

"There's nothing more we can do," doctors told the family. They indicated that if she did come out of the coma, she would be noncommunicative because of irreparable damage she had suffered. They felt it was time for them to say their goodbyes and think about disconnecting the respirator.

Audrey's immediate family, her church family, and her Christian women's group continued to pray. Feeling it just wasn't time yet for Audrey to go, they notified every prayer chain and ministry they knew in the U.S. to pray for her healing. Close friends kept an around-the-clock prayer vigil. Praise music played in her room day and night.

Audrey's Christian women's group called a special prayer

meeting. Though a few of them had heard something about Audrey being "brain dead," they didn't discuss this extremely negative report. Ten women began to intercede, offering worship and adoration to God and asking for a healing touch for their friend. Several times they said aloud, "Audrey, come back." Two members of the group who arrived late had started their intercession while still in the car. They, too, were praying, "Audrey, come back."

Shortly after this prayer meeting, Audrey's daughter asked a doctor to remove the respirator. "While we respect your opinion, we know a doctor who is higher than you," she said. "My mother will not die, but live."

When Audrey was taken off the respirator, she began to breathe on her own but irregularly. They took her off medications, but she continued breathing. Her eyes fluttered, she began tracking movement around the room, and then her mouth moved.

On the third day she squeezed a hand in response to a question. Soon her right toe moved, then her right leg, followed by her left. Most wonderful of all, when she opened her eyes she knew everybody and was "in her right mind." Thankfully, she had no memory of the terrible pain she had endured.

Audrey began months of rehabilitation to regain her strength and learn to walk again. At last she was able to return to her Christian women's group as their speaker. Walking carefully with a cane, but erect and robust, she stood and told them about a beautiful, clean, holy, peaceful place she had visited during her hospital ordeal.

"I saw beautiful angels all around—myriads of angels—and all of them were focused upon a brilliant white cloud," she recounted. "From this cloud I saw a hand extended, and I heard a voice, majestic and grand beyond description. The voice said, 'Audrey ... you must go back.'"

Her prayer group excitedly told her that all of them had been praying in agreement and saying to her spirit, "Audrey, come back." They were overwhelmed with joy and thanksgiving that God had restored her. Today, Audrey's ministry in her church and in the outreach of her women's organization is more dynamic than ever.

Long-Distance Prayer Partners

Miriam, who lives on the East Coast, wrote us about her two prayer partners—one in the South and one in the Midwest. She calls on them for prayer when troubles arise in her family.

"But often they are calling me before I have a chance to call them," Miriam said. "The Lord uses them back to back in my life—often on the same day for the same problem. Once when I was overwhelmed with problems with my two young adult children, my prayer partners called. 'How's Mandy? What's Frank up to?' they asked.

"We began to pray, and God began working mightily. Mandy, who was pregnant, was protected from her boyfriend beating her and causing a miscarriage. Frank is getting ready to move again because of disobedience, but God keeps calling him back to Himself. I know He has a purpose for each of them to fulfill, and He's not going to stop dealing with them. I thank the Lord for prayer partners with discernment."

Praying for Children's Mates

Paula and her prayer partner Jerene, who met when their older daughters were ten years old, began praying together with other women whose children went to the same Christian school. After a few years the two of them zeroed in on praying together once a week for their four children. Jerene had a girl and a boy, and Paula had two girls. Though they were still young, the two moms prayed diligently every week for their children's future mates.

"We were drawn to the passage about Abraham's servant who went to seek a bride for Isaac," Paula said. "He sat down by a well at the time the daughters of the townspeople were coming out to draw water. Then he asked God to let the girl who offered a drink of water to him and to his camels 'be the one you have chosen for your servant Isaac' (Gn 24:14). We prayed that our children would marry only the one God had chosen for them, and we asked God to keep away the wrong ones. My husband, Greg, agreed with us on this prayer."

Paula and Greg's older daughter, Nicole, was seriously dating a young man in the last year and a half of high school. The relationship lasted into her first semester of college. Both parents were certain this was the wrong match for their daughter, so they prayed the relationship would not last.

"While in prayer during Nicole's last year of high school, Greg believed the Lord gave him assurance that she and her boyfriend would break up the following year," Paula said. "He felt she would have a different group of friends by then, and that after their breakup, the boyfriend would do things to disappoint her. Because of this she would not be tempted to go back into the relationship."

In September Nicole started college. Paula, her husband, and her prayer partner prayed hard. One morning as Paula sat out on her screened porch, she said, "God, you have to tell me something."

When she opened her Bible to Isaiah and began reading chapters 42 through 46, God spoke to her through many verses, including these: "Do you question me about my children, or give me orders about the work of my hands? ... What I have said, that will I bring about; what I have planned, that will I do" (Is 45:11b; 46:11b).

"Then it seemed He whispered to me, 'The man of my purpose will come,'" Paula said. "At that moment I knew it was a settled issue. Within a few months Nicole and her boyfriend broke up. A year and a half later David, 'Mr. Right,' walked into her life, and they were later married."

The same month she met David, Nicole wrote a college Bible study article and picked Scriptures for that month. They were the exact verses God had given to Paula, plus one more: "See, I am doing a new thing! Now it springs up; do you not perceive it?" (Is 43:19).

"Jerene and I were elated, and so was Greg," Paula reported. "As each of our children reached the age of marriage, God has been faithful to bring just the right spouse into that child's life. Now we are beginning to pray this prayer for our grandchildren."

Although these two moms are now separated by hundreds of miles, their prayer partnership continues as they pray together by long distance.

Multiple Victories Through Prayer

Sarah shared a story of God's intervention through her prayer partner, Cheree, whose family owned a motel and restaurant in their town.

"My rebellious sixteen-year-old, Shane, had been drinking and trying drugs, and finally moved out to live with his father," she said. "One night he and a group of his friends checked into Cheree's motel to have a party, and Shane signed the hotel registration. That night another praying friend of mine was working the front desk. She recognized Shane and warned him about getting in trouble with the law."

As soon as he left to go to the room, the friend called Sarah, who in turn called Cheree. All three began to intercede fervently for these kids. Shane had second thoughts and left the party. Within a short time police squad cars surrounded the room and arrested everyone in it. Shane was implicated, but because he had left, he was not charged. A coincidence? These three intercessors certainly don't believe it was.

After moving to another town, Sarah met Mildred, who has been her prayer partner for seventeen years. "We are very different from one another," Sarah said. "We don't do much together except to pray, but God really has knit our hearts together. We are honest with one another, exhort one another, and pray faithfully for each other's family and needs. When we share a need it goes no further than to God. That is something we agreed on years ago."

Sarah and Mildred have seen one husband come to Christ and be delivered from smoking and drinking. Another husband, now deceased, made it through four major surgeries with no problems when doctors said he couldn't survive even one without difficulties.

"Once we prayed for Mildred's daughter to be healed of hyperactivity, and she was able to quit taking her medicine," Sarah reported. "That miracle took place seventeen years ago; the woman is a very calm young mother now. Other times Mildred prayed with me for the finances for two overseas prayer journeys. Both times I received miraculous provision."

Six years ago the Lord awakened Sarah early one morning to pray for Mildred. "She had been ill but seemed to be better. I couldn't imagine what the emergency might be," Sarah said. "I instantly sat up on my bed, pointed my finger in the direction of her home, and commanded her to live. Within a few days, doctors checked her again, diagnosed the problem they had missed earlier, and performed surgery. Though she should have been very ill afterward, she wasn't. The doctors said her healing and recovery were remarkable. God had already prepared the way for her with victorious, commanding prayer! This experience really increased our faith."

These stories illustrate the powerful results of partners praying in agreement. But always the enemy tries to lay traps for us. In the next chapter we'll take a look at the vulnerable side of prayer partnerships.

Chapter Eight

Avoiding the Pitfalls

Be self-controlled and alert. Your enemy the devil prowls around like a roaring lion looking for someone to devour. Resist him, standing firm in the faith.

1 PETER 5:8-9a

Stay alert for pitfalls when someone asks you to pray in agreement with them about a matter. We must be sure the prayer is in agreement with God's will, based upon His Word—not motivated simply by our own selfish desires.

One time at a retreat on the West Coast, I (Quin) had spoken on prayer, mentioning the power of agreement. Afterward a strikingly beautiful blonde came up to ask for prayer.

"Pray in agreement with me for my husband," she said.

"What is his name?" I asked.

"Oh, I'm not married," she answered. "But I moved here a few months ago because I believe God told me I'd find my husband here. I received a prophecy that my ministry won't go far or be very fruitful until I'm married. I want my ministry to flourish. And I want to be married."

"Sorry to disappoint you, but I cannot pray in agreement with you for this," I told her. "I will pray for God's plan and purpose to be accomplished in your life. But I haven't had opportunity to pray about your situation and ask God for His leading as to whether I should pray you will find your husband in this town. I just cannot come into agreement with such a prayer request."

The woman looked shocked and hurt because I would not pray specifically for her husband to come forth—from wherever he was. But I stood firm. The point is, it's important to be careful what we pray for. We're always scripturally safe to pray for God's destiny for someone, and to ask the Holy Spirit to reveal His will for that person. After all, Jesus taught us to pray, "Thy kingdom come, thy will be done on earth."

Guard Against Counterattack

Sometimes in the midst of a prayer battle we're fighting, we come under attack. It may be a health problem, a financial setback, an accident, or some other crisis that makes us stop and say, "Whoa—I need to ask God (and myself) a few questions":

- Am I on the right prayer assignment?
- Do I have adequate prayer coverage for the type of spiritual warfare I've undertaken?
- Have I moved outside my own sphere of spiritual authority?
- Have I opened a door to the enemy through unforgiveness or some other sinful attitude?
- Do I need a different prayer strategy?
- Have I missed God's timing?

Our friend Lorie asked herself all those questions when she took on a risky prayer assignment and then ended up almost losing her life. She and her prayer partner Jan had prayed together for years, particularly targeting each other's children. One day Jan called Lorie with an urgent prayer request. She had just learned that her son wanted to marry a former sweetheart, now newly divorced, who was already pregnant with his child. In addition, the young woman and her family were involved with a major cult.

As a result of prayer, the couple went to Jan's pastor for counseling, who agreed to marry them. After the wedding, Jan, with Lorie's prayer support, tried to talk to her new daughter-in-law about the dangers of her false religion. There was no visible response, but Jan felt she was planting seeds of truth.

Lorie researched books and Internet resources to learn all she could about this religion, then shared her findings with Jan. They wanted to be more on target as they prayed for the daughter-in-law and others caught in this web of deception. About this time Lorie was scheduled to take a trip with her daughter, and she learned that on their return flight they would have a layover in the very city where this cult group has its headquarters.

Surely this must be a divine appointment, she thought. Before leaving on the trip she told Jan and her pastor, "I'm going to pray against that false religion right at its main source."

After a wonderful vacation time together, Lorie and her daughter started their journey home. When they arrived in the city that was her prayer target, Lorie walked around the airport praying that God would "take down the control center of this false religion and deliver the people from their deception."

Just before catching her connecting flight, Lorie took a bathroom break. The minute she walked out of the rest room, she collapsed and passed out. An ambulance transported her to the nearest hospital, with her daughter at her side. When all the doctors' probing failed to pinpoint the reason for her severe pain, her daughter demanded an MRI. The test revealed she had suffered an aortic aneurysm, and doctors rushed her to surgery.

Her daughter immediately called home to alert family members, and to ask Jan to put Lorie on every prayer chain she knew about. Her mother's life was in danger. When Lorie finally opened her eyes, she was on a ventilator, with all kinds of tubes connected to her. She had received four blood transfusions and had an incision stretching from the bottom of her breastbone to her lower abdomen. But she was alive.

The irony was that Lorie ended up spending three weeks in a hospital operated by the very cult she was praying against. When they tried to proselytize her, she firmly stated her faith in Jesus Christ and the veracity of God's Word, and they never brought up the subject again.

"I received excellent care, and I never felt that I was going to die," Lorie said. "But I did ask God why it was necessary for me to go through all that pain. I was reminded that my body is flawed—as all bodies are—because of man's fallen nature. I know that no one survives something like this without passing what I call 'God's law of when'—when He has something else for us to do."

Lorie recuperated for many months and has now almost

regained her strength. She feels sure the Lord gave her an assignment to pray, but now realizes she should have had more prayer coverage before trying to take on such a major cult in its headquarters city. Now she is back to praying with Jan on the local level for people who are involved in this group. Meanwhile, the daughter-in-law has agreed to have her new baby baptized in Jan's church, where they were married. "That is definitely an answer to prayer," Lorie concluded.

Guard Against Judgment

Sometimes parents who have prayed in agreement for years for their children suddenly stop praying following a child's divorce. They wash their hands of former in-law children.

One such couple dealing with this painful issue prays daily for their ex-son-in-law to have a heart of appreciation and gratitude, not of greed and manipulation. And they ask God's blessings upon him.

Another praying husband-wife team admitted that when their daughter-in-law left their son for another woman they had a difficult time praying for her. At first they allowed their personal hurt and disappointment to color their prayers. They had fallen into a pitfall of judgment, condemnation, even bitterness.

Then one day they realized that because their two grandchildren lived with the mother and her woman companion, they had an even greater obligation to pray for their former daughter-in-law. One Scripture captured their attention: "When you stand praying, if you hold anything against anyone, forgive him, so that your Father in heaven may forgive you your sins" (Mk 11:25).

Not only did they want their sins forgiven, they wanted to extend forgiveness to her—it was a choice, not something they felt emotionally. They prayed for God to give her wisdom in rearing the children; for her to have a considerate and compassionate heart; for her to allow the children more visiting time with their dad and grandparents; that she would allow them to attend church; and that she would not adversely influence them into thinking that her choice of lifestyle was one they should choose, too.

"By praying for our grandchildren and their mother, we are hoping also to stop the cycle of prodigal behavior," the grandmother told us.

Guarding Your Heart and Honoring Others

In a group where both men and women are present, it's acceptable for a man and woman to pray together for a specific need. Or for a mixed group of three or more to "partner" together for times of prayer. But it is a mistake to establish a long-term prayer partner relationship with a person of the opposite sex other than your spouse.

In a mixed team going on a prayer journey or missions outreach, you must be extremely cautious in your conduct with a member of the opposite sex. This is the time to "abstain from all appearance of evil" (1 Thes 5:22, KJV). On more than one occasion, members of the opposite sex serving on the same prayer team have fallen into sin because they were careless in this regard. One pastor left his wife and family and was forced to resign his church because he felt it was God's will for him to marry his new prayer partner.

A young woman we'll call Cheryl made a mistake, though innocently, when she enrolled in Bible school shortly after becoming a Christian. She began attending the optional early-morning student prayer meetings and met a young man from Asia. He came to her one day and asked if they could become prayer partners, and she agreed.

Over the next few weeks they gathered in the auditorium with other students for the early-morning prayer meeting. Sometimes they would find a quiet corner in the prayer room where they could pray together with more privacy. Cheryl was oblivious to the fact that this young man wanted to spend time with her for more than just prayer. Then one day he said to her, "I've been praying about this, and I believe God wants you to be my wife."

Cheryl was shocked and dismayed, because she had no romantic interest in him whatsoever, yet she didn't want to hurt his feelings. He had read much more into her friendliness and willingness to pray with him than she intended. Finally she told him no as gracefully as possible and said they shouldn't pray together anymore. It was an embarrassing and painful lesson for a young Christian to learn.

As intercessors get involved or "caught up" in prayer-partner relationships, they need to guard their time. One pitfall is failure to judge the appropriate amount of time spent with a prayer partner or support group. We've heard of intercessors whose families felt neglected and resented the blocks of time the person spent away from them. Finding a balance may be hard, but it needs to be a priority, especially for some long-winded pray-ers. No doubt, many of us would rather pray than cook, clean house, or do laundry. But even while working at home doing menial tasks, we can do our individual praying and not fail to care for our families.

On the other hand, we need to be extremely sensitive when God's called us for a prayer assignment. We need to be willing to lay aside other activities temporarily, asking Him to reveal His will for us as an intercessor.

Know Your Sphere—Stay Focused

"Intercessors are not immune from having God's agenda crowded out by that of the world," writes John D. Beckett. "It is an enormous challenge to know how to focus—to discern between that which is appointed and that which is likely very good, but is unappointed."

Beckett suggests:

Know your sphere. What is your sphere in prayer? Is it American youth? The condition of the church? The political arena, the arts, or media? It could be the recovery of our cities. Maybe it's as specific as a particular family or individual. Or focusing on God's purposes for Israel and the Jewish people. Or on our nation's capital. How large or small our sphere is, is not the important issue. Faithfulness to that calling is.[1]

In the Scriptures you'll notice Jesus' emphasis on focus. Being aware of how easily distracted we are prone to get, he admonished, "Seek ye first the kingdom of God" (Mt 6:33, KJV). And in the parable of the sower he refers to distractions as "the cares of this world" (Mt 13:22, NKJV).

Remaining alert and watchful will help us stay focused and balanced in our prayer times together. Some conversation is necessary to help us zero in on prayer targets, but we must guard against gossip and idle talk that steals our prayer time. That is a trap the enemy always tries to use against prayer partners.

Prayer Lists

One friend who visited a church's prayer group for the first time found their "list-praying" style very uncomfortable. As a spontaneous type of pray-er, Sue was taken aback as she sat listening to each woman seated in the circle praying in turn for the first name on the list. Then each one prayed for the second person listed, the third, and on and on until all ten of them had prayed through the list of a dozen or more people. Two hours later she left bored and frustrated, even doubting that she'd been praying in agreement with them.

Were the church women wrong? Not necessarily. This was their traditional way to pray, and they had grown accustomed to it. Sue's spontaneous, conversational type of prayer may have been so foreign to them, it just wouldn't work in their group. We must be careful not to judge Christians who pray differently than we do. Some are "list pray-ers" and some aren't. In group settings it's best to fit in with their traditional style until you get better acquainted and can offer suggestions for variety in a nonoffensive manner.

However, if you are considering being "yoked" with a prayer partner as a long-term arrangement, it's advisable to pray together a few times to determine whether your different styles are compatible. Not that they have to be identical. But each should be comfortable with the way the other person prays and not be offended if the partner wants to introduce new ideas for prayer.

Remember the picture of the symphony orchestra! The two of you may be as opposite in style as a trumpet and a violin, or a tuba and an oboe. But if you're both "on the same page," so to speak, and following the conductor, your partnership can be effective.

Barbara tells a story of teaching at a Bible school in another country when the president of the school insisted that every student arise at 4:00 A.M. to pray for one hour over the list he had compiled the day before. The students were discouraged and bored. But some admitted that if they came across a prayer request that touched their hearts, they'd have no difficulty praying with great zeal for it, and time would not be an issue. She feels it's usually best for list pray-ers to pray independently. Those with a need for diversity find praying another person's list inhibiting, confining, and boring.[2]

Still another pitfall is allowing one person to do all the praying— either in a group or in a two-person partnership— without giving others an opportunity to participate. We know some "silent pray-ers" who would rather not pray aloud before others. But at least allowing time for them to pray is a courteous consideration. To avoid this trap, develop the habit of pausing after a few sentences of prayer so the other person has a chance to speak up.

Many of us have sat in meetings where we heard elegant prayers and thought, "I wish I could pray like that." Since I (Quin) grew up in a church where I heard only the pastor pray aloud on Sunday mornings, I had a hard time learning to pray aloud at first. I had to get used to hearing my own words spoken.

The truth is, eloquent prayers are not required. Pouring out our hearts in our own style and manner of speaking is what moves the heart of God. Prayers packed with faith are what's needed to get the job done. So let's do away with intimidation, keeping our prayers and thoughts God-centered, avoiding the pitfall of trying to impress others. We may never have an impressive vocabulary or become an orator. But our Father, who created each of His children uniquely different, loves to hear us talk to Him.

We all want to avoid pitfalls in our prayer life. So let's ask God to link us up with just the right prayer partner, and then heed Paul's admonition:

Put on the full armor of God so that you can take your stand against the devil's schemes.... And pray in the Spirit on all occasions with all kinds of prayers and requests. With this in mind, be alert and always keep on praying for all the saints.

EPHESIANS 6:11, 18

Chapter Nine

Lessons From the Field

Let us hold unswervingly to the hope we profess, for he who promised is faithful. And let us consider how we may spur one another on toward love and good deeds.... Let us encourage one another.

HEBREWS 10:23-25

A wonderful benefit of having prayer partners is that we learn so much from one another's experiences, as well as from our mutual study of Scripture. In this chapter we share a variety of stories sent to us by teams of pray-ers. They will enrich your own experience as you seek God's direction with your prayer partner.

Never Give Up!

Sometimes our prayer partners join us in praying for family members for months and years without seeing results. Then suddenly—after what seems like an eternity—the answer comes. But eternity is exactly what our praying is about.

Lorna had prayed a long time for her mother to accept Jesus, but Josie steadfastly refused. In fact, she wasn't too pleased when Lorna went away to Bible school. And she didn't want to hear anything about Lorna's Savior. "Religion," as she called it, turned her off.

Lorna became concerned when her mother got sick and doctors didn't know the reason. Then the tests came back one Thursday. Cancer. That same day Lorna went to stay with her mother, and early the next morning asked if she could pray with her. This time Josie agreed.

"I prayed with her for forty minutes, binding the spirit of fear and asking God to permeate her with His peace," Lorna said. "I walked her through forgiveness, then had her repeat a prayer acknowledging that she was a sinner in need of Jesus' forgiveness and healing."

Surprisingly, Josie did it all without protest. After praying, she repeated the name "Jesus" over and over several times.

"Lord, if it's her time to die, please let it be without pain," Lorna prayed silently. Josie was weak but experienced no pain, even though her body was riddled with cancer. On Sunday night Lorna crawled up beside her mom on the bed to watch *Touched by an Angel* on television. The two cried together as they watched the program about a father who had a hard heart toward his son. At last Lorna felt that her mother's hardened heart toward her had melted. Later that night Josie died peacefully in her sleep.

How quickly Josie's life ebbed away after her diagnosis! How soon she slipped into eternity and into the arms of the Lord she'd so recently accepted. With great joy Lorna shared the good report with her prayer partners, who had faithfully stood with her through those years of praying for Josie.

Praying From a Distance

About a year after Barbara became a Christian, her husband was transferred to a city in Texas, where they bought a new home. One day loneliness overwhelmed her, so she went for a bike ride in her new neighborhood. When she noticed someone had just moved into the same model home as her own, she jumped off her bike and knocked on the door.

"Susan opened the door, and I welcomed her to the neighborhood," Barbara said. "She invited me in, and we sat in her kitchen visiting like we'd known each other for years. Looking around the room I saw many Christian plaques, so I asked, 'Are you a Christian?' I was so excited to hear a 'yes' in reply."

Over the next three years the two became close friends and prayed for each other regularly. When Barbara's husband got military orders to move to Korea and later to the Philippines, she specifically asked her new friend to be her prayer partner. Susan committed to pray for Barbara whenever the Lord would bring her to mind. Then Susan, whose husband also was in the military, got transferred to Hawaii.

"Each time I crossed the Pacific, I was able to stop off in Hawaii to visit and pray with Susan," Barbara said. "We just picked up like we'd never missed a beat. Years later we moved to northern Japan, and Susan and her husband moved to southern Japan. We prayed together over the phone regularly and didn't even have to pay long-distance charges, as the U.S. military had special telephone connections. We also attended Protestant Women of the Chapel retreats together."

Amazingly, ten years after they had gotten acquainted, both families moved back to the homes in Texas where they first met. They began walking together to visit and catch up on events, and pray for each other's families. Soon they were walking and praying over the homes in their neighborhood every day.

"We saw great breakthroughs in the families of our neighborhood," Barbara said. "Now that we live in separate states again, we correspond and pray via e-mail and telephone. And on special occasions when I'm in Texas, we get together to pray face to face."

Mentoring a Younger Prayer Partner

Myra, a seasoned prayer warrior, says God always seems to link her up with younger women as prayer partners. Usually she becomes their mentor in prayer, just as an older woman had done for her.

"Back in the 1970s I asked for a prayer partner, and God gave me one near my daughter's age," she said. "We met once a week to pray. That pattern has continued in my life for twenty-five years, though the partners have changed because of my moves."

Her current prayer partner, Donna, is about twenty years younger than Myra. They pray on the phone daily, usually after Donna's children are in bed. "We pray for spiritual situations in our families, as well as for significant world events," she said. "Recently Donna's husband was put in jail. He had neglected to pay speeding tickets he'd received, and some small checks had bounced because foreign travel and long hours on his job made it hard for him to keep their checkbook in order."

First, Myra and Donna asked God for direction on how to pray. They felt it was OK to pray that his boss not find out he'd been arrested, and that he'd be able to pay his fines and get released. As it worked out, that's what happened. But the two women experienced some long periods of intercession before a successful conclusion came. In the end, Donna's husband assured her that he wouldn't be careless like that again. It was a learning experience for all of them.

Myra lived in a variety of countries during years of service with Youth With a Mission, so she has the nations on her heart. She spends hours a day interceding for specific countries, and sometimes joins with a prayer partner by phone, e-mail, or letter to pray in agreement over conditions in various parts of the world. Often she gets a prayer assignment while watching the international news on television.

"Praying with younger women gives me opportunity to encourage them in their Christian walk and to mentor them in ways to pray more effectively," Myra said. "But we shouldn't become dependent on just one prayer partner, or allow another person to become dependent on us. God is our source, and we must rely on His love and acceptance of us."

Unexpected Answers at Unexpected Times

Even when we pray for people only occasionally, God is faithful to honor those prayers, often answering at unexpected times and in unexpected ways.

Dot, who had been adopted as an infant by a maternal aunt, found out after she was grown that the person she had known as "Aunt Marie" actually was her birth mom. This woman wanted to establish a mother-daughter relationship, but Dot wasn't very interested in the idea. By this time, she and her husband had moved thousands of miles away.

"Aunt Marie would write and try to get me to acknowledge her as my mother—but I just couldn't," Dot said. "My parents were good parents; they put up with me, fed me, clothed me. My husband and I occasionally prayed for Aunt Marie, but she was so difficult to get along with, we usually remembered her only on her birthday and at Christmas. When I would write and tell her interesting things about our children, she responded by sending me pages of instructions on how I should raise my kids. Poor dear, she felt she was teaching me. If we sent her a gift, she rarely liked it; she really was a cross old lady."

One year, while attending a relative's funeral back in her home state, Dot felt she should go see Aunt Marie. She convinced a cousin, Shirley, to go with her, though she wasn't sure whether she was a "praying cousin" or not.

"When we arrived at the nursing home, I told the lady in charge that we wanted to see Aunt Marie," Dot said. "She suggested we meet in a small room where we could visit privately, but Marie said, 'No, we will meet right here.'

"When Shirley and I went into this large room and sat down to visit with her, a man sitting next to her listened in on our conversation. Aunt Marie turned to Shirley and asked, 'What church do you belong to?' Upon her response, Marie said, 'I belong to the same denomination.'"

At this point Dot said, "Aunt Marie, it doesn't matter what church you belong to. What really counts is whether you have invited Jesus to live in your heart."

As quickly as Dot had said that, Aunt Marie replied, "I accept Jesus as my personal Savior."

The little man sitting next to her said, "And so do I."

As Dot tells it: "Two souls came into God's kingdom that day. I never saw Aunt Marie again. She fell and broke her hip and died the following year."

Her story illustrates that prayers of agreement for someone who needs salvation—even as infrequently as she and her husband called on God on behalf of Aunt Marie over the years—are not in vain. The Holy Spirit had prepared Marie's heart, and Dot's visit was the catalyst for her to receive Christ. As for the cousin who went along on the visit, who knows what seeds were planted in her heart that day?

God Redeems Our Mistakes

Upon learning that her adoptive father had cancer of the larynx, Dot was concerned about his spiritual condition. She knew he had never made a commitment to follow Jesus. With her husband backing her up in prayer, she flew to her parents' home for a visit, hoping to talk to her dad about the Lord. But her visit started off all wrong. Early in their conversation Dot remarked, "Dad, we are all sinners."

"Well, I'm not a sinner," he retorted. So Dot backed away from the subject.

Later, when an old friend came to visit, she and Dot went out for coffee, and Dot shared her concern about her dad. They bowed their heads and prayed together right then—asking God for direction.

Back at home Dot found her dad watching a TV program that was anti-Christian. "Dad, you don't want to listen to that—those people are in a cult," she said. Surprisingly, he didn't object to her statement.

"We talked about it, and I told him how the 'real Jesus' died for our sins," Dot told us. "Then I asked him if he'd like to know that he could go to heaven with Mom and me someday. He immediately nodded yes."

Dot explained some principles from the Bible, then asked him to repeat a prayer after her. Her mom and dad prayed the sinner's prayer together. He'd had his larynx removed and had to speak with a vibrator that he held up to his throat.

"He put the vibrator down, got up and danced around the room," Dot reported. "He felt such relief that he would be going to heaven! He lived five more years, then had a fatal heart attack. But his was a true commitment, and I know we'll be together someday because of it."

Short-Term Assignment

Jill is a friend with a host of prayer partners, but she shares an experience of linking up with people from other parts of the world for a specific, short-term prayer assignment.

"One year in the fall I moved to Jerusalem for three months," she wrote. "While there I knew the Lord wanted me to fast and pray for forty days for the nation of Israel. I partnered with two wonderful individuals—Charles from South Africa, and Mary from the Philippines. In the natural, we were an unlikely combination. But in the spiritual, God connected us 'at the hip,' so to speak."

During that forty-day period, the three prayed and worshiped the Lord for at least ten hours a day. They prayed not only for the nation of Israel but also for each of their respective countries.

"The unity in the Spirit and the bond of love that we developed continues to this day," Jill said, "even though we're not necessarily permanent prayer partners. We saw daily personal answers to prayer and experienced incredible grace to do a water-and-juice fast for those forty days. It was a life-stretching experience, and I will never be the same!"

Mentoring a Prayer Partner

Melissa shared with us how she became partners with her now close friend Penny.

"God called me to be an intercessor," she wrote. "He also has anointed me to 'hear' prophetically and to sense things He is doing. This gifting works consistently, especially when I'm praying with Penny, whom I led to the Lord.

"Penny got my attention when I realized she was involved in some occult activity, not realizing that she was in spiritual error. I grieved over her in prayer for weeks, then voiced my concern to a mutual friend. 'Don't worry about her,' the woman said. 'She's looking for God's truth, and when she sees the real, she will drop the counterfeit.' That is exactly what happened."

One day, out of the blue, Penny called Melissa. In listening to some tapes on the dangers of New Age teaching, she had become fearful that perhaps these warnings applied to her.

She asked Melissa to clarify things for her.

"I've always found that if I know what God has spoken in Scripture, I can better judge what someone claims is a vision, dream, or prophecy from God," Melissa told her, choosing her words carefully.

She encouraged Penny to read God's Word on a regular basis, and also to read Christian books she loaned her on various topics, including a book that presented the reality of spiritual warfare and demonic activity. Penny became increasingly excited about the things of God as they unfolded for her. When the two women with their husbands attended a gospel meeting together, both Penny and her husband renewed their commitment to follow the Lord.

"Little by little, she began to let go of the counterfeit and hold on to the real," Melissa remembers. "One day Penny asked me which objects she should remove from her home that might be displeasing to the Lord. I felt the Holy Spirit cautioned me not to respond as I usually would have. 'If you pray, God will be faithful to show you what is of Him and what is not,' I told her. Over time Penny removed from her home various objects related to her former interest in occult matters."

After a while, Melissa felt the Lord's urging to teach Penny a greater depth of prayer. It helped a lot that Penny took a Bible school correspondence course and became more grounded in the Word of God.

"We began to pray once a week, then twice a week," Melissa continued. "Our respective spiritual gifts worked together perfectly, as we prayed together for our family members. Many times her prayers helped rescue my family from various disasters, and God has honored our prayers together in countless other situations."

Penny has grown spiritually and learned quickly by having a mentor. "In praying together, Melissa and I tap into much more power than when we pray apart," she shared. "I've been a Christian for eight years, but she's been one almost thirty years. She's not only my prayer partner but my spiritual mother."

Journaling Your Prayers

Our friend Joyce shared with us how the Lord has sometimes led her to keep a prayer journal for friends she has prayed for as they faced challenges in their lives.

Recently Linda, a pastor's wife whom Joyce had been meeting with for prayer, learned that her daughter was pregnant before marriage. Linda had just weathered several family crises, and this news devastated her. Joyce had been through a similar experience and had great compassion for Linda's pain and disappointment.

In prayer one day she felt the Lord say, "Write down the prayers you pray for her." So Joyce began a prayer journal for Linda. This nine-month assignment covered the time from when she first learned of the situation through the six-week postpartum period.

The daughter soon married the baby's father, and by the time the little boy was born, everyone happily received this precious gift into the family. Joyce visited the new mother in the hospital and prayed over her infant son. Six weeks after the baby's birth, she gave Linda the prayer diary.

"God wants you to know that He 'had you covered' during this difficult time," she told the new grandmother. "This is a record of His faithfulness to you." The diary aided Linda's healing as she experienced God's peace in a new and deeper way.

"I am not sure all the reasons journals have been important," Joyce reported. "But they have been a discipline for me to pray consistently, and a tangible way by which God shows His steadfast love to the recipients. I pray for a number of leaders, but I only keep a journal of prayers for an individual when God specifically directs me to do so."

Once it was for a prominent woman leader in South America whom Joyce had met on a missions trip. For a full year she prayed and wrote her entries in English, and at the end of the year sent the journal to her new friend. Joyce later learned this woman had had every word translated into Spanish so she could read it easily. (See appendix for principles of prayer journaling.)

One Seasoned Intercessor Trains Another

Each morning at 7:30 before Pam goes to work, she drops by JoAnne's house for a twenty-five-minute prayer session. They don't drink coffee or discuss the issues of the day. Sitting in JoAnne's living room with Bible and prayer lists in hand, they "come boldly unto the throne of grace" with key issues (see Heb 4:16, KJV).

Pam, twenty years younger than JoAnne, wanted to learn a deeper form of intercession from a seasoned prayer warrior, so JoAnne has been mentoring her for the past six years. They always start their session acknowledging God—naming His wonderful attributes—and worshiping Him. Then they launch their prayers for their city, state, country, other nations of the world, and the Jews. They bless the city fathers—from the mayor on down to the firemen, and also the state officials.

JoAnne does most of the praying while Pam adds her *yes* in agreement. They pray for key evangelists around the world—that God will enable them "to bring in a harvest of souls," for God to extend His protection and provision to them, and that the new converts will grow in their relationship with Christ by having *disciplers* to help them mature in the faith.

"We also pray for the persecuted church around the world," JoAnne said. "We pray for those Christians who are going to be martyred today—that the glory of God will be on them and that they will feel no pain. If they are not to be martyred, we ask God to give them a way of escape.

"I don't miss a day without praying for the salvation of Jews around the world and for the peace of Jerusalem, and for my own country to have righteous leaders," she said. "We also pray for wisdom and protection for those responsible for our local schools, as well as for the students and their families."

JoAnne is a key intercessor for her city's prayer task force. Since they began praying for their community, they've seen nude nightclubs closed and public video game rooms outlawed. Today, forty-seven churches in their community and county participate in twenty-four-hour prayer watches. Each congregation takes one twenty-four-hour period each month. Since there are more than thirty-one churches in the prayer covenant, several double up on the same day—thus the area is blanketed with prayer around the clock every day of the year. Because JoAnne is the intercessor who stands behind the main facilitator for this prayer project, these two pray together over the phone on a regular basis.

For the past three years, a prayer rally has been held in the civic center just before school starts. Each school has representatives there, with bands and choirs participating as prayers are offered for all the schools for the coming year. City officials and pastors from various denominations also attend and participate. (See appendix for the blessing prayer they pray over their city.)

These stories attest to God's faithfulness and show us that when people began praying together, it becomes contagious. As answers come, people are encouraged to continue praying and to get other believers involved. They learn that prayer—far from being dull or boring—is one of the most thrilling activities they can give their time to.

Keep in mind that we serve a God of miracles. When we do the possible—which is to be obedient to pray—God will do the impossible.

Chapter Ten

Passing the Flame

In all my prayers for all of you, I always pray with joy because of your partnership in the gospel from the first day until now, being confident of this, that he who began a good work in you will carry it on to completion until the day of Christ Jesus.

PHILIPPIANS 1:4-6

M ore is caught than taught," the old saying goes. How true this is in imparting prayer to the next generations.

Usually the idea of passing the flame brings to mind the Olympic Games, when runners carry a torch across the nations every four years and ignite a flame at the opening ceremony. But when we refer to passing the flame in a spiritual sense, we're speaking of a much more important contest than any athletic event. It's the eternal destiny of a generation.

Not long ago I (Quin) climbed in the car with my older daughter for a day of errands and shopping. She turned to her two toddlers in the backseat and said, "Let's pray together now." They folded their hands and held them under their chins while she prayed for peace, safety, protection, direction, and a good day. She asked God to station angels about them, then thanked Jesus for dying for them. When she finished, they all three said "Amen" together. Then she cranked the car to leave.

She is passing the flame of prayer to her young children. And she does it at mealtime, at bedtime, or whenever they are starting off somewhere in their car. She often creates processional worship banners for her church while the children play at her feet.

I feel this daughter has outdistanced me in prayer. She's stood before hundreds and prayed aloud, unashamed and with holy boldness. Her influence in passing the flame of prayer has enlarged as she leads a weekly two-hour prayer session for Israel once a week at the World Prayer Center in Colorado Springs. She fell in love with the nation of Israel at age thirteen when I took her there for the first time, and later she lived there during four short-term assignments. Several times a year she brings dedicated prayer warriors to her home for further prayer for Israel.

Winning the Battle for Our Children

But this firstborn daughter of mine wasn't always a prayer warrior. Our children had been in church with us since they were infants, but during the renewal of the 1970s, when all three were in elementary school, LeRoy and I were radically changed. We asked the Lord to help us establish a truly Christian home and started family devotional times. We encouraged our children to keep prayer journals and to pray aloud, even as we were learning. I remember clearly the time each one stood publicly in a church and invited Jesus into his or her heart.

Then came peer pressure, some rebellious years, days away at college when we didn't know what was happening in their lives. This only drove LeRoy and me to even more concentrated prayer! I spent hours digging through the Bible to find God's promises for our family, asking the Holy Spirit to teach us. I listened to the prayers of pastors, leaders, and godly women, even writing some of them down. I was after something big—getting hold of God and seeing my prayers answered and my children set free.

LeRoy and I prayed together daily, asking God to forgive us for mistakes we'd made as parents. We knew God's enemy and ours, Satan, was trying to keep our children in his camp. But we had God's promises, and we stood on them. Others joined us in our five-year prayer battle.

Then within months of each other, all three recommitted their lives to Christ. Of course, we have continued to cover them with prayer through each stage of their lives, and now we seek to leave a legacy of prayer for our six grandchildren.

Mother and Son Pray in Agreement

One Christmastime, after our son Keith had graduated from college, he asked me to suggest a book he could give to his best friend, Mark, to answer his intellectual questions about Christianity. They had been longtime neighborhood chums and classmates.

We searched for just the right book, though I can't remember the title. Then Keith and I agreed to pray together for Mark until he came to Christ. This was long-distance praying, as Mark, Keith, and I were all living in separate cities at the time. Mark would write to Keith with his questions—sometimes phone him—and I backed Keith up with prayer. Finally, after several years, Mark acknowledged his need and made Jesus the Lord of his life.

We kept praying for Mark, as he had some rough tests along the way, and some great disappointments. A few years ago he fell in love with a girl he met at his job; soon she accepted Christ and became a radical believer. Today they're happily married.

Recently he was in our city to address a group of leaders as a consultant, and Keith brought him by the house for a short visit. Since I'd seen him only once since high school graduation, I sat amazed as Mark talked about his church, the things of the Lord, and his commitment to his wife. I thanked God for this answer to the prayers of agreement my son and I had prayed more than fifteen years earlier.

When I learned he had received a standing ovation for the speech he'd given at this business gathering, I couldn't help but say, "God's grace and favor is upon you, Mark. He is the one who has given you these talents and opened doors for you."

"I know," he agreed. "I know it's Him."

Mother-Daughter Prayer Partners

Our friend Kayla wrote us about her experience of training her young daughter to become her prayer partner. Here's her story in her own words.

I had prayed for years for my husband, Ron, to become my prayer partner. He was a Christian, but just didn't feel comfortable about praying with me except when we prayed for our children.

One Christmas Day, while my eight-year-old daughter and I were alone, I felt the Lord said to me, *Lay hands on your daughter and pass your gift of intercession to her.... Start praying with her.* Lisa had asked Jesus into her heart at age five and had always been open to talking with me about spiritual matters. She learned very quickly as we began praying together about school problems, her friends, and the usual stuff.

I wanted to join a group going on a prayer journey to Israel to celebrate our tenth wedding anniversary, but Ron wasn't interested. So Lisa and I made it our prayer project. We prayed for almost a full year. When she asked from time to time, "Has Daddy said yes yet?" it was hard to disappoint her. But I felt strongly that the Lord wanted us to go, so we kept praying. Finally Ron agreed. The day I told my little prayer partner, "Daddy said yes!" her face lit up with the biggest grin I'd ever seen. Both of us learned a lot that year about perseverance and walking by faith. And the trip was a life-changing experience for Ron and me.

Three years later Matt, Lisa's older brother, tried to commit suicide at age seventeen. It was she who found the suicide notes on his bed when she got home from school. Lisa was twelve at the time, and home alone because Ron and I had gone to look for Matt. As she ran through the house crying, praying, and wondering what to do, the Lord spoke to her: *Sit down and wait—your parents will be home shortly.* If she hadn't been trained to pray and listen, she wouldn't have been able to hear the Lord speak at such a traumatic moment.

Ron and I arrived about twenty minutes later and got a call from the hospital saying that Matt had driven his car off a cliff, but had been rescued and brought in by helicopter. What a comfort, as we raced to the hospital, to reach to the backseat for Lisa's hand and pray with her all the way during the twenty-five-mile drive. The hospital staff gave us a private room to wait for the doctors' report, so Lisa and I sang and worshiped and prayed together the whole time.

After the tests I stayed with Matt, praying through the night for his recovery. Ron and Lisa drove back home. But it was Lisa who prayed and read Scripture to her dad to bring him comfort, instead of the other way around. Through prayer, treatment, and therapy, Matt had a remarkable recovery. During those months of recuperation, Lisa was Matt's encourager. He often felt freer to talk to her than to his dad and me.

Soon after this, Ron at last became my prayer partner, although Lisa and I continued praying together until she went away to college. She has been on her own for three years now, and I know that her first job and many other breakthroughs in her life have come through prayer. Truly, she has developed into a mature, godly young woman. I'm so grateful I obeyed the Lord and trained her to be my prayer partner, despite her youth.

An Extended Family Prays Together

While there are probably numerous families across the country that pray together on a regular basis, we know one particular family that has consistently observed a once-a-week prayer time for years.

Don and Denise share a home with their son Andrew and his wife and two children. On Mondays, during "family night," they discuss the week ahead and any special prayer requests any of them have. But they don't limit their praying to Monday nights. One year when school opened, Denise's granddaughter was getting sick every day while in class. The family began praying in agreement against the anxiety that was causing her illness. Soon she improved.

Andrew, the music director at his church, called his wife and parents to pray specifically during the time he was in a special meeting with the pastor. The meeting went smoothly as the two were led by the Holy Spirit in their discussion of the church's worship agenda.

"Our praying together is a lifestyle—a communication system that is open twenty-four hours a day," says Denise. "We have a multigenerational commitment as we pray for and with my in-laws who live on the West Coast. When my mother-in-law comes to spend the winter with us, we have four generations praying together at our house."

Monday nights are reserved for family prayer time—no one plans any other activity on that night. Few households have as many generations living under the same roof as this one does, but many couples do share their prayer needs with children, parents, or grandparents via phone, letter, or e-mail. Prayer can be the glue that holds the extended family members together.

Let the Children Pray

Someone once said, "The most intimate relationships we ever have are with our families—those we grew up with and those we make for ourselves later on in life."

Parents, then, have an awesome responsibility, both to teach children to pray and to pray with them.

Esther Ilnisky, who heads up the Children's Global Prayer Movement, believes parents have a critical role in mentoring their children by teaching them to pray from the time they can talk and then releasing them to become prayer warriors for God.

She writes:

> If youth and children are now making up half the world's population, then I believe half the Christian world's prayer warriors should be youth and children. Godly children are the most untapped resource of prayer today, both in the home and in the Church worldwide. Nurturing the prayer potential of children could free them, free parents and free the Church from the very fears for them that cause us all such grave concern. Equipping and liberating them to use godly authority over evil powers could transform them, you, your home and the Church and could ulti-mately revolutionize the world.[1]

The National Children's Prayer Network draws youth each year to Washington, D.C. for their own prayer congress while adults observe the National Day of Prayer. Lin Story, the network's founder, wants to challenge youth of all ages to recognize their prayer potential.

Karen Moran, of Children's Global Prayer Movement, said, "I see God beginning to explode in the children—showing them their giftings, and that the same things that Jesus did and that adult ministers do, they can do, and the Holy Spirit doesn't have an age."[2]

Jerry Lenz, who develops children's teaching materials, points out that children need outlets to share their faith. "If they don't have opportunities, they become like ripe fruit that's not harvested—and they can die on the vine." That's why he believes involving kids in outreach, evangelism, and prayer is vital.[3]

We need to involve our children in our prayer efforts. In addition, we need to keep encouraging them, speak blessings over them, and let them know God has a destiny for them. Only God knows what will happen if we Christian parents pray for our children and leave footprints of faith for them to follow as we obey this Scripture: "We will tell the next generation the praiseworthy deeds of the Lord, his power, and the wonders he has done.... so the next generation would know them, even the children yet to be born, and they in turn would tell their children" (Ps 78:4, 6).

Different Prayers for Different Kids

In her book *When Families Pray*, Cheri Fuller suggests:

If your children feel that praying aloud is awkward, hold hands as a family, pray silently, then end by having someone read a verse aloud. Or have each person write down two prayer requests; exchange lists in the morning, then pray for each other during the day.

You can also connect kids' interests and prayer. Sports-oriented children can thank God after a win and pray for a good attitude when they lose. Musical children can sing Scripture prayers set to music or make up original song-prayers. Artistic kids love to draw things they want to say to God, and verbal kids love praying Korean-style, where everyone prays aloud at the same time.

Give your children room and grace to be who God created them to be. Encourage them to try different styles of prayer and watch them take off![4]

Grandparents Provide Prayer Models

Grandparents, as well as parents, can provide prayer models for children in a society where intergenerational bonding is so badly needed. Not only can the younger ones hear their grandparents pray, but they can come to expect their prayers when needed. I (Quin) pray with my preschool grandchildren whenever the opportunity arises. When they spend the night with us, I enjoy our evening discussions before final kisses and prayers. They each pray aloud after I do.

The other day when four-year-old Evangeline got stung by a bee three times, my son Keith called me so she could ask me through her sobs to pray away her pain. Of course I prayed right then over the phone as she listened. In fact, I was joining my prayers with Keith's, who at the moment was struggling to comfort her.

Last month I was sleeping across the room from five-year-old Lyden Benjamin when he awoke from a nightmare. "Mama Quin, how do I get those monsters to go away?" he asked, sitting upright in his bed.

"Just tell them in the name of Jesus and because of His shed blood, they have to go away—and I will agree with you," I answered.

"Oh, OK—is that all?" he asked. I prayed and he repeated after me, then he rolled over and soon fell asleep again.

"Grandparents have the opportunity to pass on the experience-based wisdom that is missing in the lives of young people ... and they can serve as a spiritual catalyst to the younger generation," wrote author and college president Dr. Jay Kesler.

After spending a lifetime in youth work he observed: "Young people who succeed in life are often surrounded by support systems, caring parents, extended family and grandparents who care." In contrast he noted that many youth who have been in trouble with the law "are ones who do not have parents and grandparents praying for them.... I'm making a passionate call for recommitment to Christian grandparents. The whole weight of responsibility cannot rest on an individual set of grandparents or a single grandmother or grandfather, but we can 'stand in the gap' in our particular situations, as God asked in Ezekiel 22:30."[5]

Passing a Prayer Mantle

When I (Quin) was invited to speak at a women's retreat at my former church in Florida after a twenty-year absence, I was

plenty nervous. After all, many of the women who had mentored me in the things of the Lord would be in the audience.

At the end I spoke on how God puts other people in our
lives, emphasizing that His divine appointments are better
than any we could arrange ourselves. At our table I was surrounded by a few cherished "best friends" from years ago.
During my speech, I paid them tribute and had each woman
stand as I told what she had imparted to my life.

Mary Jo had been my mentor for many years, since the first
day she brought her team of women from her church to
redecorate my home, using things I already had on hand. On
that morning long ago, Mary Jo and five others—all strangers
to me—sat in my living room praying that as they redid our
home, it would reflect our family's personality and God's
glory. When they finished, it did. Mary Jo was the first to
encourage me to give ten-minute Bible study talks at her
women's meetings. Her extravagant love and caring is so real,
she's never missed sending me a birthday card in thirty years!

Sitting beside her was Margaret. For six years she and her
husband were part of a weekly couples' prayer meeting in our
home. We had sown prayers into each other's lives and families. She also made my curtains, taught one of my daughters to
sew, and the other to bake bread. Though now a widow, she
still reaches out in love to younger women.

Next was Lib—my prayer partner who had prayed faithfully
with me every weekday at 8:00 A.M. for seventeen years with
our prayers focused for our husbands and our seven children.

Babs had stood in some tough prayer gaps with me—and I
with her. I remembered the times we had wept in each other's
arms as we prayed for her son, who is still in prison. But now

we rejoice about his walk with Jesus, even in his tough situation.

Liz, a businesswoman, was mostly my "let's have some fun" friend—teaching me not to take life so seriously. Since both our husbands had their pilot's licenses, we'd taken a few small plane excursions together. After I'd moved, she flew their plane, solo, to visit me. Sometimes when the men took our children for weekend flying trips, she and I drove to nearby Orlando for church and lunch. Now the other prayer partners and I join our prayers with Liz's as her husband suffers from a brain tumor.

After I thanked each woman for her part in my Christian growth, I sat down as lunch was about to be served. A young woman approached our table to speak to all of us "older women."

"We younger women, sitting in the back of the room, heard how you have been friends all these years—even when one of you moved away," she said. "It touched us all to hear how you've continued to pray for one another. We made a covenant today to do the same. We want to have lifelong friendships like you've had, and pray for each other, too. Thanks for a great show-and-tell lesson!"

As she turned to leave I noticed most of us "oldies" had tears in our eyes. I realized I had come full circle. I was blessed to be surrounded by precious women who had spoken into my life, who had invested time praying with me and for me when I was a mom with three young children. Along the way they modeled Christianity before me.

Here I was, a grandmother, encouraging a younger generation of women who love the Lord to follow our example. In a sense we older ones were passing a prayer mantle to the younger ones that morning—imparting to them a bit of our experience. Asking them to carry the torch to the next generation.

We say to you, our readers, "Come on, women, you can do it. Take time for prayer partners. Take time for friendships. Take time to help each other with your homes and your children. Pray for God to give you the people of His choice to walk beside you in your Christian pilgrimage."

Ruthanne and I are trusting God to show us how to complete his assigned task for us in our generation. Is that your desire, too? You can count on one thing: God has called you to pray for certain individuals in your lifetime. Maybe you won't know until you get to heaven how important those prayers were, or what was accomplished because you were faithful. So don't give up—it is always too soon to quit!

You may want to stop and pray, "Lord, don't let me miss Your purpose for me. Show me how to pass a prayer mantle to the next generation. Help me to be faithful to pray for those You've placed in my life. I ask in Jesus' name, amen."

Appendix

1
Suggested Warfare Prayer for Children

This is the prayer Barbara and her husband prayed for Lisa (see chapter 5):

"In the name and under the authority of Jesus Christ, my Lord, I bind all principalities, powers, and spiritual forces of evil in the heavenly realm exerting influence over my child[ren] __[name them]__. Your assignments against them are cancelled by the blood of Christ.

"I bind and break spirits of witchcraft, occult activity, satanic interest, mind control, fantasy, lust, perversion, rebellion, rejection, suicide, anger, hatred, resentment, bitterness, unforgiveness, pride, deception, unbelief, fear, sensuality, greed, addictions, and compulsive behavior. [Add others the Lord reveals.] I break their power and the power of rock music, and I declare them null and void in the lives of my children. The blinders the enemy has put on my children must go, in Jesus' name. My children *will* see the light of the gospel of Christ; they shall be taught of the Lord, and great will be their peace (see Isaiah 54:13).

"Father God, Creator of all things, I thank You for the gift of my children. I ask You to dispatch angels to watch over them and protect them in all their ways (see Psalm 91:11). I ask You to send Christian friends into their lives to help them and be a godly influence. Lord, what an awesome privilege and responsibility to be a parent. Help me discern when my children need my prayers or my help. Give me wisdom to be the parent I need to be, and help me to be an understanding friend to them.

"Father, may my children fulfill Your plan and purpose for their lives. May the Spirit of the Lord be upon them—the Spirit of wisdom and understanding, the Spirit of counsel and of power, the Spirit of knowledge and the fear of the Lord (see Isaiah 11:2). I release these gifts You've given me, Lord, and I place my children in Your hands. Thank You that You love them more than I do, that your plans for them are plans for welfare and peace, not for evil, and that you will give them a future of hope (see Jeremiah 29:11). Amen."[1]

2
A Prayer for Blessing Our City

Father, we bless this city with a spirit of wisdom and revelation in the knowledge of Jesus Christ, and with a thirst and hunger for revival. We bless its leaders with a spirit of wisdom and revelation and with a knowing of the times, like Israel's tribe of Issachar. We bless its churches and ministers with the bold utterance of the gospel, with faith to move mountains, with unity, and with a mighty open door for ministry here.

We bless families here with biblical structure—love for God and each other, humility, commitment to traditional marriage, and to the sanctity of motherhood and life. We bless children and youth with a spirit of obedience and respect and godly growth.

We bless this city with racial harmony and unity that will be an example to other cities. We bless the media with a love of truth and unbiased reporting. We bless the cultural and social services with wisdom, strength, and finances to meet many needs. We bless businesses and professions with integrity and prosperity. We bless our schools with godly education, peace, and harmony. We bless our law enforcement, military, firemen, and rescue workers with courage, protection, and honor.

We bless this city with great revival, and a trust and reliance on God. We release these blessings in the name of Jesus Christ and we declare this is one city, and one nation under God.[2]

3
Principles of Prayer Journaling

Our friend Joyce shared with us some of the principles she has learned with journaling prayers:

1. It seems the Lord directs me to keep and give prayer journals to people who need extra encouragement and the undergirding of His inescapable love and care. He may lead me to keep a journal when the prayer target person is struggling with loneliness or extreme spiritual battles.
2. An assignment like this is a sacred trust, and anything God reveals to me or that the person shares with me must be kept in absolute confidence. I don't want to make the person's trial more painful because I didn't keep a confidence.
3. Timing is important. The Lord helps me know how long to keep it, which prayers to write, and when or if I am to

give the journal to the person who is my prayer target. As with other matters of guidance, if the journaling is done for a longer or shorter period of time than He directs, it will not produce the desired fruit.

4. Keeping the journal sharpens my spiritual hearing, and always increases my love for the person I'm praying for. It brings me closer to seeing the person as God sees him or her.

5. I am transformed as I pray and write. If my heart is cloudy with sin, I cannot hear His voice. It also disciplines me to have quiet times with the Lord. Sometimes I have felt I was hearing Him clearly only when I was praying and writing in intercession for someone else. As I wrote and prayed, I gained new strength to go out into my world and trust Him with my own problems.

6. Strong, deep friendships have been a surprising but wonderful benefit of this type of consistent praying. Whether or not the person knows I am keeping a prayer journal, it is as if the bond of friendship is being woven in the Spirit with giant knitting needles.

7. Journaling this way helps ingrain the habit of steadfast prayer. After the assignment is over I find that I'm in the habit of seeking Him and praying on a more consistent basis. Prayer journaling may be the Lord's way of training me, as well as seeing that important assignments for prayer are covered.

4
List of Prayer Ministries

Aglow International
P.O. Box 1749
Edmonds, WA 89020

Lydia Fellowship International
P.O. Box 4509
San Jose, CA 94040

End-Time Handmaidens, Inc.
P.O. Box 447
Jasper, AR 72641

Global Harvest Ministries
P.O. Box 63060
Colorado Springs, CO 80962

Love Your Neighbor
P.O. Box 2247
Charlotte, NC 28247

Moms In Touch
P.O. Box 1120
Poway, CA 92074

MOPS (Mothers of Preschoolers) International
1311 Clarkson St.
Denver, CO 80210

Houses of Prayer (HOPE)
P.O. Box 141312
Grand Rapids, MI 49514

Intercessors for America
P.O. Box 4477
Leesburg, VA 20177

Every Home For Christ
P.O. Box 35930
Colorado Springs, CO 80935

Esther Network International
854 Conniston Rd.
West Palm Beach, FL 33405

Mission America (Lighthouse Movement)
5666 Lincoln Dr., Suite 100
Edina, MN 55436

Suggested Periodicals

Pray! Magazine
P.O. Box 469084
Escondido, CA 92046

Global Prayer News
Global Harvest Ministries
P.O. Box 63060
Colorado Springs, CO 80962

Intercessors for America Newsletter
P.O. Box 4477
Leesburg, VA 20177

SpiritLed Woman Magazine
600 Rinehart Rd.
Lake Mary, FL 32746

Notes

Chapter 1
The Power of Agreement

1. W.E. Vine, *Vine's Expository Dictionary of Old and New Testament Words* (Old Tappan, N.J.: Fleming H. Revell, 1981), 43.
2. Jack W. Hayford, ed., *Spirit-filled Life Bible* (Nashville, Tenn.: Thomas Nelson, 1991), 1624.
3. Jack Hayford, *Prayer, Spiritual Warfare, and the Ministry of Angels* (Nashville, Tenn.: Thomas Nelson, 1993), 98.
4. Jack Hayford, *Daybreak: Walking With Christ Every Day* (Van Nuys, Calif.: Living Way Ministries, 1984), 70–71.

Chapter 2
Finding the Right Prayer Partner

1. Dutch Sheets, *Intercessory Prayer* (Ventura, Calif.: Regal, 1996), 80.

Chapter 3
Making Your Spouse Your Prayer Partner

1. Prayer based on Isaiah 11:2; Luke 2:52; Colossians 1:10; Isaiah 54:13.

2. David and Jan Stoop, *When Couples Pray Together* (Ann Arbor, Mich.: Servant Publications, 2000), 46–47.

3. Kathy's story is shared in more detail in *When Couples Pray Together*, 129–31.

4. Stoop, 79.

5. Stoop, 79–80.

6. Elizabeth Alves, Barbara Femrite, and Karen Kaufman, *Intercessors: Discover Your Prayer Power* (Ventura, Calif.: Regal, 2000), 43–44.

7. Stoop, 144–46.

Chapter 4
Learning Prayer Principles

1. Adapted from our book *A Woman's Guide to Getting Through Tough Times* (Ann Arbor, Mich.: Servant, 1998), 198.

2. For detailed teaching on the principles of spiritual warfare, see our books *A Woman's Guide to Spiritual Warfare* and *The Spiritual Warrior's Prayer Guide* (Ann Arbor, Mich.: Servant Publications, 1991 and 1992).

3. Al Novak, *Hebrew Honey: A Simple and Deep Word Study of the Old Testament* (Houston, Tex.: C&D International, 1987), 143–44.

4. Sheets, 99.

5. Tommy Tenney, *Answering God's Prayer* (Ventura, Calif.: Regal, 2000), 23.

Chapter 5
Faith Building 101

1. Maria's story first appeared on pages 227–28 of *A Woman's Guide to Breaking Bondages* (Ann Arbor, Mich.: Servant, 1994).
2. Helen Kooiman Hosier, *100 Christian Women Who Changed the 20th Century* (Grand Rapids, Mich.: Revell, a division of Baker Book House, 2000), 25.

Chapter 6
Praying With Vision and Expectation

1. Mary Lance Sisk, "Love Your Neighbor As Yourself—Restoration of Your Neighborhood" (cassette tape distributed by Aglow International, Edmonds, Wash., 1995).
2. New video "How to Pray for Your Children" by Quin Sherrer is available through Gospel Light, P.O. Box 3875, Ventura, CA 93006 or by calling 1-800-4-GOSPEL.
3. Adapted from revised edition of *How to Pray for Your Children* by Quin Sherrer with Ruthanne Garlock (Ventura, Calif.: Regal, 1998), 71–73. Used with permission.
4. Quin Sherrer and Ruthanne Garlock, *A Woman's Guide to Spirit-Filled Living* (Ann Arbor, Mich.: Servant, 1996), 228–29.
5. Steve Hawthorne and Graham Kendrick, *Prayerwalking* (Orlando, Fla.: Creation House, 1993), 15–17.
6. Hawthorne and Kendrick, 126–30.

7. Reported in *Pray!* November/December 1999, 31–32.

8. Alvin Vander Griend, *Intercessors for America Newsletter*, March 1999, 2. Mr. Vander Griend is director of HOPE (Houses of Prayer Everywhere); 1-800-217-5200.

9. Griend.

10. Adapted from *The Lost Art of Intercession* by Jim W. Goll, (Shippensburg, Pa.: Destiny Image, 1997), 64.

11. Paul A. Cedar, "The Lighthouse Movement," *Pray!* November/December 1999, 18.

12. C. Peter Wagner, *Global Prayer News*, Volume 1, No. 1, January/March 2000, 1.

13. Quoted in *Pray!* Issue 20, 2000, 46.

Chapter 7
Distance Doesn't Matter

1. Goll, 99.

Chapter 8
Avoiding the Pitfalls

1. *Intercessors For America Newsletter*, June 20, 2000, 1–2.

2. Alves, Femrite, and Kaufman, 42–43.

Chapter 10
Passing the Flame

1. Esther Ilnisky, *Let the Children Pray* (Ventura, Calif.: Regal, 2000), 33–34.
2. Cheri Fuller, "Big Things Happen When Kids Pray," *Charisma*, September 1998, 43.
3. Fuller, 46.
4. Cheri Fuller, *When Families Pray* (Sisters, Ore.: Multnomah, in association with Alive Communications, Colorado Springs, Colo., 1999), 112.
5. Jay Kesler, "Grandparenting: The Agony and the Ecstasy," *Focus on the Family*, March 1999, 2–3. (Adapted from Dr. Kesler's book by the same title published by Servant, 1995).

APPENDIX

1. Quin Sherrer and Ruthanne Garlock, *A Woman's Guide to Spiritual Warfare*, 160–61.
2. Sent to us from South Carolina praying women; used by permission.